PRAISE FOR *THE MASON HOUSE*

"In this graceful and moving memoir, Bertineau offers a series of stories about love, tenacity, resilience, and hope from a rare corner of the world."

—M. Bartley Seigel, author of
This Is What They Say

"Touching and authentic."

—Faith Sullivan, author of
Good Night, Mr. Wodehouse

"A powerful celebration of the ties that bind us and of eccentric, laugh-out-loud moments of love, grace, and what it means to be kin."

—Tiffany Midge, author of
Bury My Heart at Chuck E. Cheese

THE MASON HOUSE

A Memoir

T. MARIE BERTINEAU

LANTERNFISH PRESS
Philadelphia

THE MASON HOUSE

Lanternfish Press

399 Market Street, Suite 360

Philadelphia, PA 19106

lanternfishpress.com

Cover Design: Kimberly Glyder

Printed in the United States of America.

Library of Congress Control Number: 2019955371

Print ISBN: 978-1-941360-43-9

Digital ISBN: 978-1-941360-44-6

For Gramma—
Not a day passes that I don't think of you.

AUTHOR'S NOTE

I was a ghostwriter of this story. Memory is the true author, or rather, *memories*—some imprinted upon me before I could even name the letters in my alphabet soup. Where I struggled to recall details, or in scenes that occurred before my birth, I relied on the recollections of my mother and siblings, as well as other family members and friends. Some dialogue—in particular, the very earliest—is a patchwork of words and phrases I recall. I reconstructed certain scenes to span gaps and provide cohesion, but such instances do not alter the authenticity of the story. I worked diligently to follow the historical order of events, but not all may be exact. Most names were changed for the sake of anonymity as well as locations modified in certain instances. Our lives are enriched by a host of individuals and events, but only those relevant to the narrative at hand are reflected in these pages.

THE MASON HOUSE

INTRODUCTION

I became fatherless in the mid-sixties. We all did, those of us who were left. Against doctor's orders, Dad was digging the car out from a midwinter storm when his heart seized. My two older sisters weren't surprised by his death, though it devastated them when it finally occurred. Months before, from the backseat of the rusty Chevy, one of them had overheard him up front confiding in his buddy. "My wife doesn't know," he said. "The doctor said I have less than a year." One sister told the other. But since it was *his* secret, they didn't tell anyone else. They just lived with the knowledge and waited.

After his death, Gramma's house—the Mason house—was our second home. Mom had lost two sons before she lost her husband. There was no end to her grief. We stayed with Gram for long stretches. A bond formed, as sure as forever.

Then one day she left us too.

PART ONE

A GIRL'S GRIEF

I arrived at Gramma's funeral dressed in someone else's clothes. I owned the scuffed Mary Janes, but the jumper was mined from the secondhands box in our utility room. I couldn't trace the tired tights. Their pilled nylon crept down my thighs, and the waistband struggled to stay around my hips, both welcome distractions. I tugged, wiggled, eyed the spring-fresh blacktop of the parking lot—unsure I was up to the challenge ahead. I knew what was expected of me. I was ten years old and skilled at hiding grief. My sisters were too. We'd had more than our share of practice. But today was different.

I tried to be strong as Mom had instructed, though a weakness diluted her words, her hands trembling, a tremor in her voice. I'd watched her struggle in life as a Chippewa woman chained to her past, much like when she swam in Portage Lake on warm summer days. She didn't slice through the water with graceful strokes and rhythmic breaths. She knew no breaststroke, no freestyle. Instead, she'd take a deep breath, draw her limbs up squarely beneath her, and off she'd go, dog-paddling her way to safety.

"How'd you learn that?" I asked her once. I was trailing along in an oversized inner tube appropriated from a stack on a local beach, quite aware I was too far from shore. Mom hadn't yet noticed. She was too busy trying to keep her chin above water.

"Your dad taught me this," she said. Her kohl eyes mellowed. She smiled at my father's memory, then sputtered as the chop slapped her face. For her, dog-paddling was a survival skill. Mom wasn't a swimmer—she couldn't have saved me then, nor could she save me now.

Knowing this about her, I understood why she needed me to stay in control—especially today. All morning I had quietly harnessed the pain. I had done a good job of it too. Until now. The moment I crossed the threshold of the funeral home on Quincy Street, a brew of odors assaulted my senses—flowers, antiseptic, death. It nauseated me. I wished I had eaten the puffed wheat my stepdad offered that morning, but I had left my food untouched. My insides could only hold so much.

Grief gnawed as we all crowded into the reception area. Ahead, large partitions were drawn, closing off the viewing room. I pressed my nose against a seam in the upholstered panels and caught a glimpse of a man in a dark suit rolling a polished box across the floor. He aligned it front and center and, as a jeweler opens a case, raised a section of the lid. Blood drained from my head. My face buckled.

No! No! That couldn't be her! There was a scuttle at my back, a sudden warmth at my side, a palm on my shoulder. I smelled Mom's wintry scent—Wrigley's from her purse and Moonwind cologne from the sapphire bottle on her bureau.

"I need you to be strong, honey," she whispered. "You said you'd be strong for Mama." She was tender but stern, and I understood. I breathed deep, hung my head, and nodded in agreement. I knew the deal. I wouldn't risk being taken home, missing my chance to say goodbye. I battened down my hatches and Mom faded into the growing crowd. There was nothing left to say.

The partitions were soon pushed aside to expand the cramped space and join the two rooms. I rushed to the wooden centerpiece, to the gleaming box with its ornate side handles and tufts of silky fabric. I peeked inside and saw her close up. My heart shivered.

So it was true. Gramma was dead.

She was gone. And I had not said goodbye, had not felt her breath upon me one last time. I had no parting embrace to remember, no touch of her warm hand. Gone were her minty eyes forever haunted by a strange, comforting sorrow—eyes that had mirrored not only my present but my past. They'd reflected our family's history, our family's pain. When I looked into them I saw myself, and I craved that even though it was sad. It was what I knew of the world, of her and me, of my dead father and two brothers who had left long before I could commit them to memory. It showed what we were as a family, and that gave me a sense of belonging. Who was I now?

I stood at her side in my castoff dress. How fancy she looked, like a porcelain doll. Untouchable. Her cheeks were faintly rouged; lips stained; fine, ashy hair washed and combed straight. It fell neatly about her neck and splayed in feathery wisps upon the pillow. Inches away, yet so far. Only months ago I'd snuggled against her, holed up in the familiar and comforting Mason house with a feeling of forever. It was late afternoon; winter was settling in. We talked that day about the past. We always did. We spoke of my real dad, her son—that's how we called my two fathers: my stepdad and my "real" dad. "He was nice, wasn't he, Gram?" I asked. "Sometimes I wish he didn't die." Through Gramma's stories, I came to know my father as the ideal man—funny, loving, kind. But I knew of him in other ways too. Through my sisters' words I knew he'd been mischievous, fallible, a romantic prone to drifting in and out of our lives. A seeker. Gramma didn't talk about those traits. She said it was wrong to speak ill of the dead.

"I wish that too, honey," she said. "Every day. I can still picture him walkin' through that kitchen door." Her gaze eased off in that direction, hopeful.

I wished I could picture him, but it had been too long. My father's face had faded, though the timbre of his voice still drummed in my chest. The scent of him still lingered. I remembered those from one cold winter night years ago in the backyard of the old rental house in Tamarack. My family had huddled there, shivering, beneath a velvet Elvis sky.

"What do you think's wrong with it?" Mom's voice wafted that long-ago night, and I lifted my eyelids to see her shadowy outline. Breath steamed dense in the silvery air. She snuggled my baby sister to her chest, a papoose[1] swaddled tight against the bite of a Michigan frost. The oil burner in the house had been acting up again, its roiling quakes threatening a strike on the night it was needed most. I was wrapped in the arms of my father, my cheek pancaked against his green shoulder, my forehead burrowed beneath his jaw. I breathed the faint odor of motor oil in his Dickies work shirt. I saw frayed threads at his neckline, like a lawn in need of a trim.

"I don't know what's wrong, but we're out now. We'll just wait." His words rumbled into me, etching their sounds into my memory. Perhaps that was what God intended, a gift he sent that night knowing that one day it would be all I would have to remember the man by.

"Do you think it's gonna blow up?" There was an edge to Mom's tone that night. She was a worrier.

"Nah. I don't think so." He hoisted me a little higher on his shoulder. My face brushed his prickly stubble. I inhaled the warm scent of his skin, a crisp wisp of his hair— Brylcreem or perhaps the night air. His chest was wide, his

---

1 Mom sometimes used the word "papoose" in jest, or as a term of endearment. It is a term of colonization. In Mom's birth language, Ojibwemowin, the word for a bundled baby is *dakonaawaswaan*.

arms strong and gentle. That had been my father, whose dire prognosis had been correct. At thirty-two, a diseased heart valve swept him away.

Gram returned her attention to me that day months ago in the Mason house, not finding what she sought at the kitchen door. Fear surfaced within me. I tasted loss. "I get scared you'll die, Gram." I locked eyes with her, which was always hard for me. "I get scared you'll leave us too." Death stole people I loved. I couldn't lose her.

"Don't be scared o' that," she said, squeezing my knee. "Gramma'll *always* take care of you girls."

Outside, sleet pelted the windowpanes, but inside I calmed. I believed her words were true. I'd always believed in her. "I'll always take care of you too, Gram."

And I meant it.

My chest ached now as I stood beside her casket. How much could a heart take? I worried about that a lot—worried my heart was weak, like my father's had been. Gram had worried too, fear etching deep canyons along her forehead and between the wispy wheat of her brows. In life, those rifts sketched her cross and disapproving. In death worry had left her. Lying there, she looked relaxed, her skin smooth, her lips drawn up slightly at the corners. A smile? She wasn't much for smiling, but begrudgingly I agreed it was better she be buried with one. My gaze trailed down to her shoulders, her arms crooked at the elbow, her hands. Everything seemed different now. There was no apron, no baggy sweater. I didn't even recognize the dress she was wearing. Where was the chocolatey brown one with the glossy buttons and windowpane check? We had a fading Polaroid of her in it. I wished she were wearing that: something familiar, something more like Gramma. But no one asked me.

Another memory festered: a long line of cars parading through Mason along route M-26, headlights winking like fairies at midafternoon. It was a funeral procession on its way to Lake Linden. Gram stood that day peeking through the wavy, yellowed sheers, hidden behind the painted window casing. She didn't want a funeral to know she was watching or to appear too interested in death. She was superstitious that way. "I don't want any of that bologna," she said. "Just roll me through town in a barrel." She had a morose sense of humor. I was used to it.

"We're not gonna do that, Gram," I said.

"Yup. That's what I want. And the band can play *Beer Barrel Polka* while they roll me along."

"*Beer Barrel Polka?*"

"Maybe youse could have a maypole…I love maypoles… with pretty ribbons and flowers."

I'd watched her that day at the window, her profile so resolute, and I'd laughed. But what if she meant it? If that's what she really wanted, then I had failed her. We all had. I always tried my best to take care of her, but I couldn't this time. I'm so sorry, Gram. I'm sorry for all this. The casket. The flowers. The funeral home.

She didn't want any of it. It was all wrong. I let her down good. Tears brimmed and guilt burned. I needed a cry. For me. For her. Mom's words swam in my head: *You have to be strong. No crying. You have to be a big girl.* My eyelids flickered. I gulped at the lump, fought back the urge—but then I had another. What if I touched her? Instead of tears. A consolation. Could I *do* that? I fixed on her hand, which lay gracefully atop the other just below her bosom. I longed to pet it, to caress her skin. Would she feel it? Would she feel *me*? My heart raced as I laid my fingers on the edge of the casket. I extended a quivering hand, whispering like a handler to a foal. "There, Gramma. You look pretty. It's all right." It seemed I hovered there for an eternity before my prickly fingertips eased their way closer to her powdered skin. Inch by inch.

The next instant, there was a voice at my ear. The spell was broken.

"No, no. Don't touch now." Great Aunty Alma swooped in smelling of Easter Mass. She patted my hand away as she plucked at the casket lining, making soft *tht thts* with her tongue as she worked. "This needs to stay real nice," she said. "Nice and pretty. Mm hmm." Her head bobbed rhythmically with the familial palsy, a tremor that had skipped over Gram.

Foiled, I watched as she tidied the satin cradling her sister. I could have done that. That was *my* job. I held my position—my stubborn streak *en garde*—but she slid around me. Her width swallowed up my view. I was forced to surrender, to accept. I'd been dismissed as Gramma's caretaker and she as mine. I was on my own now.

SOMEONE TO WATCH OVER ME

The sun lingered high over the old mining home's tar paper roof, the heat penetrating the plaster. The Mason house would be a kiln by suppertime. Four years old, I milled about the steamy kitchen while Gramma fixed us a bite to eat. My two older sisters and I had been staying with her for several days now. She took care of us a lot since Dad died; Mom wasn't doing too well. Earlier, Gram had declared we'd be having sandwiches because it was too hot to fuss with anything else. This heatwave was uncommon for Michigan's Keweenaw, a peninsula steeped in Lake Superior and cooled by her winds.

The weather was hardest on Great-Grampa Otten. He sat that day as he always did: sideways at the kitchen table, knees splayed, round belly cradled between his thighs. Gramma had opened the cellar door hoping he might be cooled by the dank air, but he still looked miserable.

"Pa, you gonna listen to your ballgame?" she asked. He was hard of hearing, so she always yelled. "It's about time to turn on your radio."

Great-Grampa Otten had moved in with his daughter years ago to help watch over her family when she became a widow, but now she watched over him. That's what families did. Like Mom, Gramma, too, had experienced loss. Her grief had gotten the best of her. She'd made poor choices, drunk too much, forgotten how to mother. Grampa's presence had balanced things out, grounding her. That's what she needed.

He responded to her question with a series of garbles that tumbled from his drooping lower lip. He'd suffered a stroke years back and for as long as I could remember had been in this condition. He could stare me straight in the eye while he spoke, but the only thing I ever understood was the word "Reka." This was his way of pronouncing my name, which was how I came to be called in Gramma's house. Beyond that, whenever he addressed me, I would look imploringly at Gramma for the translation. She understood him.

"Batter up!" she said. Baseball talk always got him going.

Grampa Otten was my first lesson in aging. He seemed ancient—a chalky cloud—and smelled like the powdery Tums in his room. A Cornishman to the bone, he dressed in long-sleeved button-up shirts with cuffed work trousers held up by suspenders. His skin loosely draped his face, and the lower eyelids formed deep *V*s in the centers that revealed the pink, glistening tissue of his eye sockets. He'd struggled with a lazy eye throughout life and, at some point, had lost his good one to an accident involving a fragment of steel.

His glass eye was notorious for popping out, an event which always made me cringe.

Once, while I sat eating at the table beside him, I heard the familiar *plink* of the prosthesis as it hit the kitchen floor. I froze mid-bite. He turned, spoke my name, "Reka," then mumbled a string of Grampa-ish sounds. Reluctantly, I edged around him, staring with dread at the cue-ball sphere that had come to a stop mere inches away on the cracked linoleum beside the wood stove.

"Reka, give Pa his eye," Gramma called from her post in the front room, where she could see the goings-on in the kitchen while watching TV.

It had never been my job to retrieve it. There was always someone else present, someone older, most often my sisters, but neither was there that day. I looked back to the floor, wondering if I could bring myself to touch it. Grampa muttered again and pinched his thumb and fingertips together like a crawdad. Still, I stood staring—a derelict. Relief washed over me when I heard the clop of Gramma's loafers on the floor as she made her way into the kitchen. Rescued!

"It won't bite," she said, baring a gummy grin in my direction. I don't remember ever seeing Gramma's dentures in her mouth, though I saw them every day in a glass in the cupboard behind the Corn Flakes. She scooped up the orphaned eyeball and handed it to him, relieving me of my duty. Grampa grumbled his thanks. No one ever asked me to pick it up again.

Baseball calling, Grampa boosted himself from the chrome-legged table and shuffled off to his first-floor bedroom. I peeked in later as he sat on the edge of his mattress, his backside sunk deep within its sprung coils, heavy oxfords planted flat, suspenders dangling loosely below his waist. I could hear the banter of announcers as they relayed the pregame events of the evening over his portable radio. He liked the local boys: the Detroit Tigers, the Milwaukee Brewers, or the Minnesota Twins.

Days passed, but the heat did not. One evening, when darkness had fallen and Grampa was asleep, my two sisters and I lounged in the big bed in Aunty Patsy's old room at the top of the steps. We all slept together on the spongy mattress, rolling inward toward the center. Even Gramma slept with us in that bed.

I was stretched out in a hand-me-down baby-doll pajama top and underpants. We had kicked the covers down to the foot of the bed but reserved the top sheet as a refuge from summer's mosquitos. Mesmerized, I watched a sprinkling of gnats flirt with the dim lightbulb overhead. Some dared to touch it, spun off into the room, and returned to the globe even more determined.

Gramma sat in a high-backed wooden chair at the window, leaning on the sill to catch a whiff of breeze from the treetops. The leaves were silent, though, with only the occasional rustling of birds in their nests or bats winging by in search of bugs. The window was propped open, its sash resting on an ill-fitting aluminum screen framed in wood. That's how the gnats homed in on the light bulb and how the mosquitos were able to feast on us in the night.

"I hate these bugs." My sister Jane slapped at her arms and swatted at her thick, black hair. She was the only one with hair like our mother, Chippewa hair. The rest of us were brunette, as our dad had been, but a deeper shade.

"It's too hot to close the window tonight," Gramma said. She tried to fix the ends of the screen closer to the window frame, though. There was a spate of clicking and scraping.

"Don't move," said my oldest sister Anne, who was focused on Janie's shoulder. She raised her hand guardedly and snapped her forearm, striking another mosquito.

"Did it get me?" Janie asked.

"I don't think so." Anne held her palm up, revealing the smashed insect but no telltale blood smear.

Beyond the window stretched night's canvas, bizarre and beautiful as a Van Gogh. Tall, indigo trees studded the yard. Branches tickled the roofline, their leaves reflecting the vast cobalt sky. From where I lay I couldn't see the palette of stars nor the periwinkle moon, though Gramma narrated their existence. She gazed wistfully out over the scene, cheeks flushed, bangs pasted to her damp forehead. Her fingers clasped the ever-present Pall Mall, thin white paper wrapped like onion skin around dried bits of russet-colored leaves.

"There's a full moon tonight," she said, voice muffled by the screen. "That's a beauty." She coaxed a tendril of smoke from her cigarette, the ash flaring silently. Chin raised, she exhaled a translucent cloud that drifted into the blue like a ghost.

"Can you see the Big Dipper?" I asked.

"I wonder if we could see the Northern Lights?" Janie added. "Dad used to say you could see them sometimes."

"Not here, though," Anne said. "Too many trees. And I think it has to be cold."

"Just moonlight," Gramma said. She was melancholy. Memories did that to her, tugging on her, pulling her out of the present. "Moonlight over Lovers' Lane." I had heard her speak of Lovers' Lane many times, though I'd never been on it. I imagined it was somewhere near the old Mosquito Road, another place she sometimes mentioned, where lovers went to smooch. She began to hum a little and then sing, still fixed on the night, one elbow resting on the sill:

Smile the while you kiss me sad adieu
When the clouds roll by I'll come to you...

Gram sang a lot. She played the guitar sometimes, too. Late in the evening, one of us girls would retrieve the chestnut acoustic from the spare room, where Dad and Mom had slept when first married. She'd shake the tortoiseshell pick from its sound hole and tweak the tuning. When her ear was satisfied, she'd strum old three-chord songs like "Hold the Tiger" or "The Sheik of Araby," often with a cigarette dangling from the corner of her mouth so she had to squint at us through a column of smoke.

She was one of ten siblings born into a musical, Methodist family. It was in her genes. Several of the Ottens had traveled the countryside performing as The Copper Country Barn Dance Group. (The Keweenaw was also known as the "Copper Country" because of its copper mining history.) Her sisters could all play piano, some of them by ear, and Gramma said her brother Will was a maestro of the banjo. Other siblings played the guitar or accordion too, and each one had a powerful voice which rang through the local Methodist churches, though Gramma was not a churchgoer herself.

Like her brothers and sisters, Gram had a passion for music. She wielded a deep alto with a lot of vibrato, perhaps from the cigarettes. The notes in her lower register resonated like the low E on her six-string, vibrating my insides clear down to my toes. She sang like a story. I loved to listen to her and to watch her sing, even though sometimes it hurt my heart. Drawn by memories, her eyes would focus somewhere in the distance on things no one else could see. Her emotions overflowed. Her longings, her losses, her regrets. They all poured out and seeped into me. Even her grief for her children—only two left now. She had outlived two daughters and her only son. I could feel it all. Even the dull toothache of her loneliness, which, try as I might, I couldn't ease.

So wait and pray each night for me
Till we meet again.

She was draped in a sleeveless cotton nightgown that hung low on her pale shins and wore white bobby socks and penny loafers. Earlier that evening, she had most likely drained her usual quart of Pabst, but the day had been sweltering and now another fat brown bottle with a long neck sweated on the floor beside her foot. She slurped the head of foam from her slender beer glass and licked her lip. "Ahh," she said. In our family, it seemed, nothing was more satisfying than a swig of cold beer.

"Why does everyone think beer's so good?" Janie asked.

"It's cold and it tastes good," Gramma said. "But you wouldn't like it. Too bitter."

"If it tastes good, we might like it," Anne said.

Gramma turned to us, eyes jade, brow wrenched. "Lips that touch wine shall never touch mine," she said. This warning was familiar. I'd heard it many times before, its tone tinged with guilt and fear. I'd long ago pledged I would abstain—I needed Gramma's kisses.

"We know, Gram," my sisters said simultaneously, ending discussion of the topic.

She shifted in the cane seat of the spindly chair, the wood crackling beneath her weight. It looked like the same chair from the black and white portrait on the shelf beside the bed, the one my father sat in as a boy. It was the lone photo in a sparse room, propped up next to the book *Black Beauty*. He was blonde then, maybe five years old. He wore a crisp, white shirt and dress shorts. It looked like a school uniform. His ankles were crossed, feet dangling, face lit by a wide, impish smile. He was luminescent—full of life and joy—precious and framed in cardboard. Few photos existed of my father, and this was the only one I'd ever seen of him as a boy. I barely remembered him anymore, but lying beside his image made me feel his presence—made me feel safer in some way.

"Girls, come here," Gramma said. "Come look."

We rolled out of bed and went to the window. I leaned against her warm shoulder.

"Look at what, Gram?" Janie asked.

"Right here." Her index finger with its truncated nail, much like my own, delicately poked the screen. A white moth flittered about on the opposite side. "There's your dad."

I peered down toward the dirt drive, not knowing what I'd see. My dad had been dead for some time now. "I don't see Daddy," I said.

"No, right here. This moth. This white one." She was almost whispering.

"I don't know, Gram," Anne said. "Why do you think that's him?"

"It hasn't flown off all night. Not like the others."

"It could be," Janie said, shrugging.

"It's him. He's checking on us—on you girls. He wants to make sure we're all right."

My sisters and I observed the moth for a little while and then returned to bed. My eyelids were heavy and my eyes stung from holding off sleep. As the sounds of my sisters' voices faded, my father's boyish face smiled down at me. Whether he was clinging to the window screen or perched there on the shelf, it didn't much matter to me. As long as he was still watching over us.

COYOTE LINGO

I knew at a young age that Gramma trusted wild animals more than she trusted men. No one told me; I learned through observation. She was ever wary of strangers knocking, keeping the doors bolted fast on both the kitchen and the shed. (The shed was a sort of mudroom between the side porch steps and the interior of the house.) At night before bed, she'd double-check the locks. *Do you want me to lock the cellar door?* I would ask when she would commence with the nightly ritual. *Yah*, she'd say. *Make sure it's good and snug.*

She taught me how to do this chore as soon as I was tall enough to reach. Since there were no locks on the door itself, I'd procure a butter knife from the kitchen drawer, drag a chrome-legged chair over, and lodge the utensil in the jamb, just in case anyone slipped in through a cellar window. Gram would always meander over afterward and test my work, just to be safe. All our door locking seemed to sum up her opinion of humanity.

Animals were another story. Gram loved them all. She had no fear of the skunks that waddled through her yard, no worries about the porcupines that scuttled beneath her porch from time to time (except, of course, where it concerned her dog's safety). She probably would have opened her door to a black bear had it chosen to knock. Once, she told me, one almost did.

In Michigan's Upper Peninsula, or the UP, as it is known, bear sightings are common. The woods are abundant and the forests deep, so there's plenty of habitat. Sometimes, our family would drive out to the local dump to watch the bears feed, just like we'd go to Lakes Drive-In on a Saturday night to see *King Kong*. Whole families of bears would emerge from the trees at dusk. They'd saunter through the brush toward the growing mound of trash, comically tumbling over one another like towels in a dryer, foraging through torn sacks and peeling cardboard. Bears were common in the UP—but they were rarely seen in town, which made Gram's story more interesting.

"I just took a dump," she said. "And was headed back up the porch steps." (The Mason house had no indoor toilet, so she was returning from the outhouse.) "I heard someone hollering my name. *Blanche! Blanche!* Eldon was across the way, waving his arms like mad, pointing."

Eldon worked at Johnson's Used Cars next door. Johnson's was a small, family-owned outfit with a gravel lot maybe sixty feet wide, a small office, and a garage with two stalls. There was always someone tinkering with cars at Johnson's. That's probably where my father fell in love with oily engines.

Gram continued. "I wondered, *What the heck is wrong with that sonuvabitch?*" She sometimes called men that—whether she liked them or not; we had to figure it out by the tone of her voice or the context of the conversation. Sometimes she spoke the word like an old Finlander, lyrically, with emphasis on the first syllable, making it seem more like a song than a swear word. Since she was fond of Eldon, on this particular occasion *sonuvabitch* was a term of endearment. "I looked where he was pointing," she said. "Holy cripes! The biggest bear you ever saw, cuttin' right through the yard for the tracks. It musta been headed to the swamp. I bet that's what panked down the switch grass at night."

"Weren't you scared?" I asked.

"Scared? Of an old black bear? No. They won't hurt ya." She took a drag from her cigarette. "He was more afraid of me than I was of him." After hearing the bear story, I rarely left the house after dark, and if I happened to be dropped off at Gramma's at night, I checked the yard carefully before climbing out of any car.

Gramma kept canaries and cats, but the pet she loved most was her dog, whom she always called "Ol' Jet-Jobber." He was a sweet and mellow thing, lean and long with a sleek black coat that swooped out in a tan, curly fringe beneath his belly.

By the time I reached elementary school, Jet-Jobber had slowed and spent much of his time asleep on the kitchen floor near the wood stove. One weekend, he wasn't at his usual post when I arrived on Friday for my visit. The house was still. Gramma looked blue where she sat in her spot at the end of the couch.

"Ol' Jet-Jobber's gone," she finally said. "I had to have him put down this week."

"Oh, sad." I sat beside her, patting her rounded shoulder.

"I called the sheriff. He came and tied him out to the tree. He was always so smart that dog—sharp as a tack. He knew what was comin'. He just covered his face with his paws." She couldn't say anything more. She snatched a tissue from the box on the back of the couch and blew her nose.

I heard the story of Jet-Jobber's death many times in the ensuing months. Whenever someone would drop by, they'd give the kitchen the once-over and ask, "Where's Ol' Jet-Jobber?" And the story would begin anew. It never seemed to get any easier for her to recount.

It was the late sixties. I was at Gramma's with my sisters, curled up in bed in the center of the parlor, where we slept in the winter to save on heating. My younger sister Katie was there too, asleep beside me. Katie didn't stay at Gramma's often. She had a disability, which made the Mason house a challenge. She'd become a mama's girl—or Mama was a Katie's girl. I'm not sure which.

My eyes flitted open that night to a commotion. Gramma wasn't in bed with us. She stood across the room, whispering to my older sisters who were awake and sitting upright. I could tell she was scared, so I got scared too. I sat up, whimpering. One of my older sisters wrapped her arms around me, though I don't recall which sister it was. "Don't be scared," she said, her breath moist at my cheek. "It's okay."

From the kitchen came a knocking at the shed door. A male voice called from the porch beyond. "Blanche? Blanche, it's me. Can I come in?"

"Who is that?" I asked.

"Shh," Gramma said. "Quiet. He'll go away." Our sentinel, she listened beside the parlor doorway, shielded behind the wall. The shades were drawn, but the room was hazy with snow's glow. I could make out her form as every so often she corralled our attention with a forefinger to her lips. Grampa Otten was asleep in the next room, but he was old and frail, his hearing near its demise. He slept on. Gramma was our only defense. I crawled to the center of the bed and pulled a point of blanket around me.

"Hello? Blanche?" said the voice. "Open the door, would ya?"

Gramma didn't budge. The knocking persisted for several minutes before the thud of footsteps descended the snowy porch. The night grew quiet again. We all crawled back beneath the covers, and I was asleep before long.

The next morning I awoke to a bright room. The shades were rolled in the kitchen and the parlor. The UP skies were overcast with their seasonal silver, but the clouds were lofty. Gramma was already up and active in the kitchen. Cupboard doors squealed and clapped, and a pan clanked as it was set to work on the propane stovetop. My older sisters were awake too, leaning against the kitchen wall just beyond the parlor doorway. Their eyes were fixed on the window overlooking the backyard and the steep-roofed outhouse—"shit house," Gram called it—a tiny, tar-papered structure planted in the snow like a birthday candle, halfway between the house and the old Mineral Range railroad tracks.

"Who do you think it is?" Anne asked.

"Not sure," Gramma said. "We'll see." She seemed more relaxed in the light of day.

I scurried out of bed and joined my sisters at the window, squeezing in from below so I could get a good view. I didn't need to ask questions. I gathered we were all awaiting something—and whatever that was, it was tied to the voice in the night. I wiggled about, my chin barely clearing the cold sill, inhaling the faint odor of lead-based, petal-pink paint. All eyes focused on the snow-shrouded hut. We waited.

Eventually it happened. The shit house door popped open—only a small bit at first, as snow had drifted against its threshold and frozen overnight. We saw it jerk once, twice, then swing wide. From the darkened shack emerged Mom's youngest brother, Uncle Ray. He was a tall stick of an Indian, a cattail, with long legs, long arms, and slim, handsome hands. His hair was mink-like and lustrous, his eyes like grape gumdrops. A stark contrast to the snowy path, he plowed his way toward the house. It was *his* voice we'd heard calling in the night, his knuckles rapping at the shed door.

"It's Uncle Ray!" Anne said.

"Your ma's Ray?" Gram paused briefly at the stove. "Christ!"

We knew Uncle Ray well—he spent a lot of time with Mom in Tamarack. She was like a mother to him too. He'd even been with us the night our father died. He'd whisked us upstairs to the bedroom, the one with the single window overlooking the drive, where an ambulance idled in the cold, red lights reflected in the snowfall. He tried to keep us occupied, tried to distract us, but our eyes wandered back to the snowy windowpanes.

"Come 'ere to your uncle," he said that night. "Stay by me, eh?" But it was too late. I saw the black mound of my father lying near the road. I stood watching beside my sisters. Their fear shrouded me.

"I hope Dad's gonna be okay," Janie said as the ambulance rolled away.

Anne was grim. She looked gray, almost old. "He's dead," she said.

"No!" Janie paled. "Why do you say that?"

"The ambulance. They turned off the lights."

Pain registered in me the night my father died—a different kind, not one Merthiolate could fix. I saw it in the faces of my uncle and my sisters. I heard it in the echo of Mom's sobs through the iron heating grate when she sat in the kitchen below us later that night. I knelt on the narrow wooden planks of the floor and peered through the black lattice. The ghostly fluorescence of a circline bulb flickered above where she'd collapsed, limp, on a kitchen chair. Mama—alone. I remember only scant fragments of my father's life, but I will always remember his death.

Mom was close with her two brothers, Raymond and David, whom we called Uncle Blue. They were Keweenaw Bay Chippewa, raised in the next county over on the L'Anse Indian Reservation. They'd grown up in a three-room house out on Dynamite Hill—isolated from other family in the nearby community of Zeba—on a plot of land allotted to them at random. (The system of allocation always sounded to me like a dreaded seating chart.) Mom said the house was built by the US government. "It was nothin'," she said. "Just a shack with no insulation." They lined the walls with cardboard and stuffed newsprint in the cracks to block the drafts. She said there was no running water, so they had to haul it in. Her papa and ma used to keep a garden and some chickens, as was expected of them. Once, they even had a cow. Mom had watched her papa plow the garden with a horse borrowed from a neighbor and felt proud. He also used to hunt bear and deer, skin the carcasses, and store the meat in the root cellar; they didn't have a refrigerator, nor electricity. She remembered a bearskin on the floor that kept her cozy. On Sundays, her ma would cook a hunk of game for dinner. Mom said she never tasted anything so good. She recalled the sounds of quiet conversation, soothing and melodic, but she didn't recall the words. "They talked good Indian," she said of my grandparents, and she was sorry she didn't. She remembered her ma going out into the woods, returning with medicines she'd harvested, steeping them for the kids.

Mom remembered good things from her early childhood, but later on the good things faded. By the time she finished elementary school, her papa had changed, grown tired. He started to do the *unexpected*. He'd always liked port wine, but now he couldn't do without it. He hunted that instead of game; the garden disappeared. Her ma came to like the wine too, and that's when the meals and the medicines stopped coming. On occasion, I overheard Mom mention it to others. *We went through hell*, she'd say. She thought I was too young to hear about it, but sometimes I did, when she spoke with her brothers. I heard bits I tried to piece together—words like "wino" and "orphanage." Once I heard Mom tell Uncle Blue that as kids, they'd lived in a dump. "We were livin' in a *dump*!" she said. A dump? I couldn't imagine! What about the bears? I hoped when I was older she would tell me the stories. Meanwhile, I worked to fill in the blanks.

Despite their living thirty miles apart, Mom's bond with her brothers was strong. They came often to visit, always bearing gifts of music. They were fun and cool and, like their older sister, resembled no one else in town. Uncle Ray had a youthful vanity about him. He wore slim pants with wide belts and shirts with wild prints. Uncle Blue was who he was: a proud Chippewa with a telltale nose and salient cheekbones. He spoke like a roll of the dice, words tumbling out in snippets, bouncing about until they found their meaning, punctuated by dry chuckles. He wore a thick, black pompadour—not at all like TV Indians—and I would sift through the coarse strands as he sat sipping coffee at our kitchen table.

"What are you doing?" Mom asked one day as I studied Uncle Blue's grayish scalp. "Lookin' for nits?" She laughed at a nervous pitch.

Uncle Blue flashed a sidelong glance. "If you find any in there, you better lemme know, eh?" Then they both laughed, an odd and conspiratorial sort of laughter. Grown-ups were always doing that; they liked to keep their secrets. After that, whenever Uncle Blue came to visit, I could always be found on my tiptoes behind him, searching his hair for nits. I had no idea what they were, but I suspected I'd know when I found one. Then maybe I'd be in on the secret too.

Both my uncles liked rock 'n' roll: Elvis, the Beatles, the Supremes. Uncle Blue's favorite was still Buddy Holly. They shared records with colorful paper labels. Sometimes they found cardboard 45s on the back of cereal boxes or got them free with purchases of Fresca. They'd plop their discs on Mom's portable turntable with the upholstered speakers and crank the volume knob. We'd all sing and dance, laughing, on the slippery oak floor of the rental house, Katie bouncing raucously on her cracked rocking pony with the screechy springs. Since Dad died, Mom herself had begun to do the *unexpected*; she had learned to numb her pain with Bosch beer. But when our uncles brought their records around, music seemed the better remedy.

"Get the heck in here!" Gramma said that winter morning when Uncle Ray reached the porch. She had already swung the door wide and was ushering him inside. "Why the hell didn't you say who you were?" She went straight to work fixing him a hot drink.

"I thought I did," he said, stomping the snow from his feet. "Couldn't you tell my voice?" He sat at the table shuddering and blowing air into his cupped hands, his almond nails neatly trimmed.

"I didn't know who the hell was out there. And I don't open that door for no stranger knockin' that time of night. Especially when I got these kids here to worry about." She gave a nod in our direction where we still stood beside the window, our mouths agape at the revolting thought of our uncle having spent the night in the outhouse.

He explained that he had hitched a ride as far as Mason on his way to Tamarack to see Mom. The snow was falling thick and blowing, and he'd thought he couldn't get any further. When Gramma wouldn't let him in, he chose to take shelter—the compost in the shit hole kept the cold at bay.

Perhaps had he been a bear, Gram would have let him in.

It was summer, the season of picnics on Forest Service tables crafted from hand-sawn logs and of long, lazy days spent on beaches along the Portage. Mom had managed to mask her grief and recently remarried—to which we were still adjusting. She left the rental house behind, though not the pain, and moved the mile or so from Tamarack City to Hubbell, where her new husband, Derry, owned a home with his mother. The marriage, for us girls, resulted in three grandmothers: our Cornish gramma; our Chippewa grandma; and now, our German step-grandma. (All our grandfathers were gone, with the exception of Great-Grampa Otten.)

Derry and I bonded early under messy circumstances. He and Mom had been out on a date. Gramma was watching us that winter evening. I was five years old. He drove Mom to the Mason house to retrieve us. They stood at the kitchen door talking. I lay on the couch bathed in the slate rays of the television, barely awake.

"Tresie's got a stomachache," Gram said. "I hope she's not comin' down with the flu."

"Uh oh," Mom said. "I better take a pail with us. Just in case."

"I'll carry her out to the car," Derry offered.

The next thing I knew, I was slumped over his padded shoulder, my cheek flat against his woolly coat, the pile collar tickling my nose. There was a descent of the porch steps, a glimpse of a yellowed incandescent bulb above the shed door. I heard the mumbling of adult voices and the wheeze of snow beneath rubber galoshes. Derry had parked along the highway, so we had to traipse up the full length of the driveway, which must not have been plowed yet. Mom trailed along close behind.

Suddenly, I turned away from Derry's collar. I needed air. My queasiness climbed. My saliva bittered. My innards hitched.

Then I puked.

I puked all over Derry, down his back onto the rich, bristly fibers of his coat.

Mom drew a sharp breath. "Oh no! All over your coat!"

"Eh, it's all right," he said. "Don't worry about it. It can be cleaned." I raised my head off his shoulder, weak from my retch, unsure the dastardly deed was complete. He faced me, grinning. I could see the white of his teeth in the purply winter night. "Feel better?" he asked, and patted my rump. There was a sincerity in this gesture—a parental competence.

In that moment, I christened him Dad.

Derry was a carpenter; originally he'd had a woodshop at the back of his mother's house. That woodshop, situated alongside the blackberry patch and the tipsy garage with the chalk drawing of a cowboy emblazoned on its south wall, became our home. He let me hang out with him sometimes while he was building it. He and a friend nailed framing and hung sheetrock, the radio blaring, echoing off the cement floor and unfinished drywall. He was eager to finish the project; he wanted to please Mom. Once, while he taped the ceiling in the kitchen, Paul Mauriat's "Love Is Blue" was playing, a catchy tune with an old-fashioned harpsichord. I looked up at Derry on the stepladder—he didn't look blue to me at all.

The wide-open space of the woodshop quickly morphed into a three-bedroom home with a small living room and a big kitchen. It was exciting to watch it take shape, to know *my* new dad knew how to do such things.

"Theresa," he said to me once when he was about done for the day. "Why 'ntcha grab that broom and sweep up some of this sawdust, would ya?"

I grabbed the shop broom propped against the wall. It towered above me and was awkward to maneuver. While he collected tools, I clumsily swept the cement, pushing all the shavings into one big pile in the center of the floor, sketching long, blonde trails behind. "Like that?" I asked when I finished.

"You make a pretty good shop hand," he said, patting my head. After that, I always tried to live up to my reputation.

When we officially moved into the shop-turned-rambler, the transition really took hold. Beer drinking aside, Derry was a good man—a funny man—but as a Korean War vet, he was strict. Katie and I were young enough to adapt easily to the new structure, and I actually liked the rules, so I didn't mind. As a matter of fact, I thought Derry was just what we needed. Anne and Janie, on the other hand, weren't so sure about the arrangement. They didn't want to replace our real dad and didn't care for Derry's rules, especially when he expected us to pitch in around the house but treated Mom like a queen; Mom had always done the cleaning before. Or when we had to help weed the garden each evening and sweep the kitchen floor every day. We even had to wash dishes after supper while Mom and Derry lay on the sofa, each with one eye open, watching Walter Cronkite on the black-and-white Sylvania on the rolling cart. Uncle Ray was a soldier now,

31

fighting in Vietnam, and Mom watched the news every night so she'd know what was happening. With all the new chores, I think Anne began to feel a bit like Cinderella. The rest of us girls took to calling Derry "Dad," but she settled on calling him just "Derry."

After the wedding, we didn't stay with Gram as much as we used to, but we still spent weekends, holiday breaks, and part of our summer with her. We had spent the most recent visit cutting paper dolls from the Montgomery Ward winter catalog (which Gramma always bequeathed to us once she had the new season's in hand); laboring behind a screaming reel mower hauled up from the cellar, its axel nearly frozen up with rust; and whacking at weeds with a sickle as dull as a soap opera. We played cards and checkers, rebuilt the puzzle with the one missing piece, and laid on Gramma as she sat on the couch, tipped on her hip, watching *Let's Make a Deal*. There never failed to be a battle over which two of us would get to lie on her big rump.

"My turn!" I said one afternoon as I dove onto the couch and snuggled up along her backside.

"Me too." Jane said, sidling up to me.

"You guys always get to lay there," Anne said. Gram's ass was broad, but not wide enough for *three* kids to rest their heads on while watching TV.

"You gotta be quick," Gram said.

As we readied for bed one warm evening, our soles black with summer's soot, Gramma retrieved the galvanized tub, which hung from a nail near the landing of the cellar steps.

She set it in the alcove between the wood stove and the wall, just in front of the cellar door. The space offered a little privacy but was drafty in the winter.

"How 'bout a bath?" she asked. "Maybe it'll cool you off before bed."

"Like swimming?" I asked.

"Skinny dipping." She gave me a wink and two quick clicks of her tongue. She filled the tub with cold water from the kitchen spigot, the only plumbing in the house, and set the silver kettle on the stovetop. When the steam whistled through the lid, she poured the hot water into the tub, warming it just enough for our baths. My sisters and I took turns bathing one by one, oldest to youngest. The water was cool and gray by the time I climbed in. I shuddered as I sank into it. I didn't like the galvanized tub, especially its pebbly ringed base. The rough, raw metal grated against my bum and the bottoms of my feet. Gram couldn't make the bath water warm enough to thwart the shivers.

Had we been in Hubbell that day, Mom and Dad might have taken us swimming *for real* in the Portage. In Mason there was no car and nowhere to swim. Though the shores of Torch Lake were just beyond the sandbank—only a short walk from Gramma's house—the lake itself was off-limits. It had been tainted by copper mining in the region, fouled by toxic levels of trace metals in the sand and barrels of arsenic and lead reportedly rusting in its depths. The Copper Country, despite all its beauty, had been ravaged by industrial pollution.

After our baths, we climbed the stairs to Aunty Patsy's old room. Gramma sat at her usual perch beside the open window overlooking the drive.

"Remember when we used to have those big weenie roasts?" Janie said. She liked to talk about the old days. "I miss those."

"Yeah," Anne said. "We'd put all the buns out on the picnic table."

"Everybody would come—"

"And we'd have sing-a-longs—"

"And play guitars…"

The Mason house had often hosted big get-togethers when my father was living. Cars would line the highway; guests would march down the drive armed with their singing voices, instruments, and beer. There would be a bonfire crackling, plenty of sticks whittled down and laden with Jet-Puffed marshmallows, and all our skin would be drenched in bug spray. Gram would cook her heart out all afternoon. She loved the weenie roasts and looked forward to the fun, but one night she passed out before the party was even over. She'd had too much beer that night and laughed so hard that she keeled right over off the porch step, where she lay, eyes closed, still as a stump, despite Janie's attempts to rouse her. Janie had heard of people "dying laughing" and feared that was what had happened to Gram. She went from one grown-up to the next. "My gramma died laughing," she said, hoping someone would help, but no one seemed too concerned.

It had been a long time since we'd had a weenie roast like that at the Mason house.

Gram sat at the window now, half listening to my sisters, half listening to the sounds of woods thick with balsam, hemlock, and ironwood. Sleep was inching nearer to me when from the sandbank along the lake came the sharp barks of coyotes. I never heard them in the daylight. Only at night, when the woods around Mason were plenty scary as it was. Those heart-plucked barks were just the beginning—a prelude to their howls, sad as a widow's wails, drowning out the leopard frogs and crickets in the slough.

"Those ol' coyotes," Gram said. "They're talkin' tonight." She leaned in close to the screen, puffed her breast, and yodeled her own string of howls.

"Gramma!" Anne and Janie giggled, as did I. "What are you doing?"

"Mark my words," she said. "They'll answer."

I lay awake, sleep postponed, but nothing. Gram let loose again, her bays sifting up through the canopy of leaves. She wasn't giving up. I'd inherited her stubborn streak, so I got it. I watched as she waited at the window, her cane seat teetering on its rickety legs. Pity pinched. Poor Gram. She looked dejected. Those dumb coyotes. Who needs 'em anyway?

When I thought all hope was lost, my heart heavy, eyes begging for sleep, at last—validation! Up from the sands, over the slough, to the thistly sky above, the lonesome song of a coyote, long and low, like the noon siren at the Hubbell firehall calling us in for lunch. Satisfied, Gram relaxed in her chair; the heart-shaped crest rail framed her head like a valentine. I looked to my sisters for affirmation, astonished and relieved. I never quite knew how to feel until I had checked with them. They were both laughing again, but not me. Not this time.

My gramma could talk to coyotes!

SHUTTER TOWN STORIES

I've read that Mason was once known as Shutter Town. The muntin windows of its quaint, white homes were all framed with board and batten shutters, each set having a unique color. It was the town Gramma moved to as a girl, the place where she married and became a widow. It was where she bore five children and grieved the death of three. She passed her days in a leased saltbox beside the highway—a Quincy Mining Company home with shutters of sage. Only a few feet from her yard, just beyond the thimbleberry patch, stood a reflective green sign with pearly block letters: "Mason," it read. It was here, in the Mason house, that Gramma wove her stories of the town's copper-mining past and the ruins it had left.

One summer afternoon, she told me the tale of Bigfoot. Rumor was he'd been seen on the Q&TL tracks, the ones high up on the ridge. Mason was once a maze of railroad tracks and trestles. Three different rail lines ran along its borders, crisscrossing one another at key locations. The Q&TL's sole purpose had been servicing Quincy's mining operation between Hancock and Torch Lake. It sat unused now, rails rusting, weeds creeping through the track ballast, though I recall the Copper Range and the old Mineral Range rails still saw a little activity.

"He came right through town in broad daylight," Gramma said of the beast as she pointed eastward. "Walked right down the highway with his red fur and long arms. He looked like a damn monkey."

"Why'd he come in town?" I asked. "That's scary!"

"Who knows? But after he passed through, all you could smell in the air was sulphur." She said he must have been hiding out in the old mine shafts—that's why he smelled so bad. I was cautioned never to wander to the upper tracks without my Aunty Lil, her younger sister, who took us for long strolls through the woods. Sometimes she'd even let us venture out onto the railroad trestle. Not too far, though, only a few feet. We'd grasp the wooden railing and cautiously pick our way from one creosote-stained tie to another. Lush, green treetops swayed dizzily in the gorge below. The upper tracks were full of adventure.

Though I was unaware of her motives at the time, Gramma's stories served to safeguard me from mining hazards. The mines had long ago closed, but the industry's footprint had scarred the landscape; there was no shortage of danger to be found around Mason. The mile-long town bordered the holdings of the Quincy Mining Company— once a powerhouse in the Copper Country—and there were ample ruins in which one might find themselves in trouble. The old stamp mill and reclamation plant were two such places, but Gramma had a solution for that as well.

"You wouldn't catch me dead going in there," Gramma said. "That timber wolf just waits up in those rafters with all that fur and those white fangs." She motioned with her fingers to mimic its sharp canines.

"Where'd it come from?" I asked. "Why does it stay in there all by itself?"

"It came down from the upper tracks," she said, pausing to strike a match. She squinted one eye as she lit a cigarette. Afterward, she shook the flame out and tossed the spent match into the ashtray on the three-legged end table. This gave her an air of casual authority on the subject, like a Perry Mason character on television. I had no doubt she knew what she was talking about. "Timber wolves are loners," she said, exhaling a long trail of smoke overhead. "They live by themselves."

The plant behind town, abandoned in 1967, was a grim structure, which at one end appeared to be sinking into the dark waters of Torch Lake. Though at some point in history many a townsman had spent his days inside its crumbling walls, I never saw anyone around the building now. Even the gulls avoided the place. Other than the echo of your footsteps on charcoal-hued gravel, the only sounds you could hear when passing by were the hollow lapping of water against the foundation and the occasional screech of steel dangling somewhere within. Beside the plant, a set of rotting railroad tracks jutted out in a circular pattern over the lake, eerie remnants of a once-bustling conveyor system. Gram said Quincy had been like a father. The company had built affordable housing, offered discounts on coal, and hosted big picnics with hot dogs and pony rides. I'd even attended the picnics when I was a tot. *They took good care of us*, Gramma would say. Those days were gone.

Like all residents of Mason, Gramma still leased her home from the company, as did two of her sisters and her brother, Cecil. Quincy might have closed up shop, but they held onto the housing. Each month she would tuck ten dollars in cash into a white envelope, lick and seal it, then hand it to one of my older sisters, usually Anne. *Don't lose it*, she would caution. Together we'd walk to the weathered gray house across from the plant—a makeshift office for rent collection.

One morning, as my sisters and I walked along the back road to the Quincy office, rent money in hand, I grew wary as we drew near the darkened plant.

"Why're you so quiet?" Janie asked.

"I'm lookin' for the timber wolf," I said.

"Gram and her timber wolf," Anne said, grinning.

Gram's stories captivated me. The images were vivid, her words spine-tingling. At times they scared me, but it was a benevolent sort of fright, like what I got from walking through the haunted house at Skerbeck's Carnival in Lake Linden. I *had* to keep listening. I had to see the stories through to the other side. And there was more to them than just good old-fashioned fear—they were educational, too. Whenever she finished a tale, I was certain I knew more about the ways of the world and what to beware of. I felt more grown up. Savvy.

"It's real," I said to Anne of the timber wolf. "Don't *you* think it's real?"

"Well, *I've* never seen it," she said, shrugging.

Mason was constructed in the late 1800s by Quincy carpenters to house the employees of its relocated stamp mill, where they crushed mined rock to extract the copper ore. Stamp mill operations had been forced away from the more populated Hancock area because they dumped too much waste into the Keweenaw Waterway (what we called the Portage canal), threatening the shipping industry. The canal had been built in the mid-1800s to further economic development of the area. It also provided a safer, shorter route for ships to maneuver across Lake Superior. Without the Portage, ships would have been forced to circumnavigate the northern tip of the Keweenaw, adding over one hundred often treacherous miles to their journey. When the US government stepped in, Quincy pulled their stamping operations off the Portage. Since mills required a water source to operate, the company shifted their location a few miles east to another body of water: Torch Lake.

The stamp mill in Mason and, later, the reclamation plant had dumped their waste rock—the tailings—into and around the lake. The coarse gray granules, known as stamp sand, diminished the lake's depth and formed enormous heaps along the shorelines. They choked out vegetation and affected aquatic life. Like desert dunes, barren and endless, the sands rose skyward and became part of the breeze. Sheets of chemically treated gravel now blew through open windows, sandblasted linens on clotheslines, and sifted through our toes in the summer. Gramma feared I would be lost in those sandbanks and told me a story of another girl who had met a similar fate. "Never play on the sandbank, Reka," she cautioned. "I don't wanna lose Gramma's girl. People get lost in that sandbank."

"What happens?" I asked, eyes wide, feet bare.

"You get sucked down. They piled it up and piled it up, but it's not solid. There's big, empty pockets underneath. Step in one wrong spot, and the whole thing could go down. *Swoosh!* Like quicksand."

Quicksand! I had seen that on TV. The thought terrified me. I bit my nails as she spoke. We both had that habit. "How do you know?" I asked.

She smoothed the skirt of her housedress while picking curls of tobacco from its threads. "Long time ago, when I was about your age, there was a little girl. Oh, she was the prettiest little thing, with blonde ringlets and a beautiful red dress."

I figured it was another story about a Finnish girl. Most Finnish girls were blonde. Houghton County was full of them. I was jealous of their buttery hair and their Delft Blue eyes like tiny teacups on a holiday table. I saw nothing similarly magical about being brown. That was the problem with growing up in that county. There were no stories about dark-haired girls—Chippewa girls like me and my sisters. You had to live in Baraga County for those, I supposed, though Gram did have a record she often played called *Running Bear*, about two young Indians who fell in love. I liked to imagine it reminded her of Mom and my real dad, though he wasn't Indian at all. In my mind, he was just a kindly white man.

The storytelling went on. "She had a little puppy who she'd play with out in the yard. Whenever she went outside her ma would say, *Never go to the sandbank*. Just as I've told you.

"One day, the girl was out playing. Her ma was busy inside. When she went out to check on her, the yard was empty. The gate to the picket fence was wide open. The girl's basket was lying beside it, but the girl and her dog were long gone."

Gram's story set off a rash of questions in my mind, not the first of which had to do with that picket fence. Which house had that little girl lived in? I'd never seen a picket fence in Mason—but Gramma had said this happened a long time ago, when she was young. There were several empty houses in town now, some dilapidated, and vacant lots too. Mason was dwindling.

"Her folks searched everywhere for her. The town came out to help. All day long they looked and looked until they finally found the puppy."

"Where was it?" I asked. "Where was the girl?"

"The dog was sitting alone out on the sandbank. The little girl's hair ribbon was close by." Gram's face clouded. Her chin dipped. "She was never found."

That story kept me off the highest peaks of the sandbank, but my cousin Lisa and I did hike around its base to pick wild strawberries or track deer from time to time. Lisa lived just down the road in the original Otten homestead—the one with red shutters. On hot days, the two of us occasionally walked along the shoreline of Torch Lake. Our bare toes would sink into the warm, slithery silt at water's edge. We knew we couldn't swim in it. We knew it was polluted, but it was *water*—a vast body of water, and it was always so hauntingly calm and quiet. All that was needed to give it life was two young girls running along its stifled shoreline, splashing with glee. One hot summer day, as Lisa and I traipsed along the beach, we got to do just that.

We were dallying behind Lisa's mom—Aunty Marjorie, or Midge, as they called her. We had joined her for a walk along the lake's western edge, which had been nearly severed from the main body of water by the enormous Quincy sands. It now formed a quaint cove behind the slough, a henna-hued kidney shape. In the gray sand behind us lay a telltale trail of footprints, a looping pattern snaking in and out like a spirograph, at times disappearing beneath the water. The stamp sand was heating up in the midsummer sun. We began to venture out further into the cove, and then a little further.

Aunty Marjorie turned and caught us wading. "Girls! Get outta the lake!"

We made a beeline for the shore, but our feet were soon underwater again. "Mom!" Lisa called to her. "Please can we go in? Just a little? It's so hot!"

My aunt turned toward us again, her hand on her hip. She appeared to be summing up the situation. We awaited her decision.

"Oh, all right. Just for a minute. But not past your knees. And don't you put your heads under that water!"

We both squealed and ran in, kicking sparkling plumes through the air, tutus of iridescence. When we were about shin deep, Lisa unexpectedly plopped down on her bottom. "Oops!" she said, laughing. "I fell in!"

I dropped down in front of her. "Whoops! Me too!" We sat there face to face, churning the water with our arms, reveling in our freedom. It was such a novelty to be cooled by the lake behind Mason. Why hadn't we done it before? We'd only used Lisa's Slip 'N Slide for that purpose.

"That's enough now!" Aunty Marjorie called from around the bend in the shoreline. "Time to get out." She must have had second thoughts.

The two of us begrudgingly boosted ourselves from the lake bottom and trudged back to shore. Never before had I submerged myself in that water. It felt strange. There was a texture to it—a density—warm and silky, unlike the Portage or Lake Superior, which were clear and cold and goose-pimple fresh. I understood then why no one swam in it, why its shores were silent. Torch Lake was dead. Mining had killed it.

THE GAME OF LIFE

Life was simple in the Mason house. Perhaps that is what I loved best about it. When the chores were done and our bellies were full, playtime was next on the agenda.

Gramma taught me at a young age how to play rummy. I learned to play solitaire by hanging over her shoulder at the kitchen table watching her slide long lines of cards from one stack to the other. "Ooh! Move that there," I said once, pointing to an open spot I thought she'd missed. Though solitaire was meant to be played alone, at Gramma's there were usually multiple players.

Gram never broke her rhythm. "That needs a red card," she said. "I have to wait and see if one comes up."

Another card game synonymous with Gramma's house was pinochle. Most everyone who knew Gram knew how to play it. Even Mom had mastered the game when she first came to live in the Mason house. Her knowledge eventually transferred to the Hubbell house, too, where she and Derry would play partners against my step-grandma and her gentleman friend, Melvin, on Saturday nights.

On rare occasions, Gram would pack up her pinochle cards and take them south to Chassell, a town twenty minutes from Mason and home of the Strawberry Festival. I liked going to Chassell. It was a small, picturesque town on Pike Bay, welcoming visitors with the tidy Chippewa Motel on one end and the Hiawatha Drive-In Theatre on the other, both sporting regal marquees. Each time we passed them I couldn't help but think that maybe if my family lived in Chassell we'd be more like royalty. Hubbell was another story. I'm fairly certain I had the only brown-skinned mother in the whole town. Grandma Woods, Mom's mother, had lived in Hubbell for a while, but when she moved back to L'Anse, that left only two other people around with skin the shade of Mom's—a cute Indian couple who lived up the road. They didn't have any kids and would walk downtown almost every day, sometimes holding hands like newlyweds. I'd be outside sitting atop a snowbank or jumping rope on the asphalt as they passed. *Hello*, they'd say with bright smiles, nodding congenially in my direction. I'd nod and say hi, eyeing them up. Once I even asked Mom about them. I burst through the back door after they'd passed by one afternoon, curious to see if my hunch were true. "Ma, ya know the Indian couple who walk every day? The ones up the hill?"

"Mm hmm," she had said. "What about 'em?"

"Are they our relatives or something?"

"No." Her forehead creased. "Why'd you think that?"

Okay, so maybe we weren't related. Yet something familiar passed between that couple and me whenever we met in

47

the road. Did they recognize that I was like them? Maybe that's why they were so friendly to me. True, I was a fair-skinned Indian, but I don't think the town quite knew what to make of any of us.

Since moving to the Hubbell house, Mom didn't talk as much about being a Chippewa as she used to. But I still thought about it from time to time. Whenever I saw my uncles or my Grandma Woods, I studied them. At Thanksgiving, our teachers would pass out coloring sheets with pilgrims and feather-headed men seated around a table eating corn and squash. I could easily see where my uncles would sit at that table. I wasn't sure about me. In Chassell—though it was still a Finnish community—at least we were a bit closer to Baraga County, where my family was more like the norm. There were traces of Indians about town. Whenever we drove through, I'd feel a swell in my chest, a butterfly feeling.

Chassell trips were the only time I ever left the house with Gramma, so they were a real treat. Gram had grown more and more distrustful of the world. She didn't like to go outside at all, but Chassell was an exception. Since she couldn't drive, some relative or other would swing by the Mason house to pick us up after supper. She'd sit in the passenger seat up front, me all alone in the back on the wide, vinyl bench. I'd watch her chat with the driver. She looked a lot smaller sitting there behind the dash, like a kid.

Gram had attended grade school in Chassell and still had a friend who lived in those parts. Pilvi was a funny Finnish woman with stooped shoulders and a tuft of white hair like froth from a spittlebug. She lived alone in a low-eaved hovel in a grassy clearing, a field that had most likely been farmed by her family at some point. The light in her kitchen was a dim ecru and the room smelled like cold, earthy potatoes. The linoleum on the floor was worn so thin it seemed there was no floor at all, as if the walls of the farmhouse had been built right onto the potato patch. They'd talk quietly together in the dusky kitchen, cigarette smoke gathering against the low ceiling overhead. I always assumed that ceiling was why Pilvi had a hard time standing up straight.

"Have a cookie," Pilvi said once when she noticed me getting bored. She held out a crackling tray of windmill cookies, their faces freckled with almond shavings. "She's really growing up," she said of me as I accepted her offer. "I bet they all are, eh?"

"Yah," Gram said. "My girls are *all* growing up." She put her arm around my waist where I stood beside her, my mouth dry with cookie crumbs. "They'll all be leaving their Gramma before you know it." As she spoke, I caught the odor of malt on her lips, a fermented haze about her mouth. I was accustomed to that scent on the breath of grownups and in the empty brown bottles they left behind.

Though Pilvi was a good card player, she was rarely a match for her longtime friend. There weren't many who could outdo Gram's card-playing skills. Even men took a backseat to Gram when it came to pinochle. I witnessed this for myself one mid-spring day when a neighbor came by for an afternoon of cards.

I awoke that morning to find myself alone in Aunty Patsy's old room. It was cold outside, but winter had passed. We had again moved upstairs to sleep for the warmer season. It was rare for Gramma to rise before me. I was usually downstairs watching *H.R. Pufnstuf* before I heard her loafers clomping down the wooden steps. My sisters weren't with me that weekend, and Grampa Otten was gone now, his room a shrine. I could hear music coming from the record player in the front room—the Statler Brothers. The song that was playing always reminded me of Gram:

> *Countin' flowers on the wall*
> *That don't bother me at all.*
> *Playin' solitaire till dawn with a deck of fifty-one.*
> *Smokin' cigarettes and watchin' Captain Kangaroo,*
> *Now don't tell me I've nothin' to do.*

I padded downstairs. In the parlor, I heard Gram set the phone receiver back on its big, silver cradle on the wall.

"Mornin', Gram," I said as she entered the kitchen. "Who were you talking to?"

"Oh, jes' Ukko. He's comin' over later for cards."

Ukko was a family friend. He lived with his folks in a T-shaped house down the road a ways. Ukko wasn't his real name—people in the UP had a tendency to assign nicknames to everyone. My Grampa Bertineau had been called Jarbo, though his real name was Lawrence Joseph. My aunt told me he had a brother named Francis, but they had called him Mikko. My real dad was Lawrence John, but they had called him Jackie. You'd think it would have been a challenge to keep track of all the nicknames, but somehow we managed.

After lunch, I went into the parlor to get a banana from the pantry closet. Through the window I saw Ukko coming down the tracks. His pile collar stood at attention around his thick neck. His chin was tucked inside his lapel, and his hands were stuffed inside the pockets of his faded field coat. The air was dense with early spring moisture as he veered off his path and waded across the vacant lot, through shrinking mounds of white and a tangled bed of bleached bottlebrush and fringed brome now exposed beneath the retreating snow. Ukko didn't walk along the roadside like everyone else—he made his own path.

Soon the thud of heavy footsteps sounded on Gramma's porch followed by a solid rap at her door. He rolled into the kitchen and slid his dampened work boots back and forth on the mat. He was a square, fair-haired Finnishman, his hairline trailing off where the ruddy skin at the back of his neck began to roll. The day's odors clung to him: damp wool, wood smoke, wet hay.

"Eh, Blanche," he said as he pulled his coat from his thick shoulders and draped it over a chair.

Gramma was already seated, preparing to shuffle the cards. I heard the familiar slap against the table as she broke the deck into two halves, then a sudden flutter, like harried wrens, as she wove the halves together beneath her thumbs. Once this ritual was complete, she plopped the deck between them on the table for the sake of fairness. Ukko cut it. Finally, the hand could be dealt.

"Is it ever gonna warm up out there?" Gram asked. "It's like the bloody Ice Age all over again." She had a lot of weather sayings. My favorite was when she called bad thunderstorms "the tail end of a tornado."

"The snow's goin' down," he said.

"One of these days I'm gonna put out some flowers—if it ever warms the hell up. Maybe pansies again. Something dug 'em all up last year."

"It'll be awhile."

I squeezed between the cold plaster wall and Gramma's chair and rested my arm on her shoulder. She was always tolerant of me hanging about. I could lay my chin on her, lean against her back, drape my arms around her. I'd never get away with that at home, but Gram was real patient. I watched in silence as the two adults picked up their cards, eyed them carefully, and sorted them by suits.

"Jesus Christ, Blanche. I got shit for a hand," Ukko said.

"I don't got much better."

"Okay," he sighed. "I'll open."

"160," she countered.

"70."

"180."

He paused and moved a card to another position. "90."

"Go 'head." Gramma jotted down the closing bid on her five-by-eight stationary pad, the one she used to write letters to her daughters. Ukko flipped the three cards in the center kitty, one by one, in a dramatic reveal. Turning over the kitty was always a big event. Those three cards were usually key to winning the hand.

The afternoon meandered along. Eventually I moved into the living room, where I lay on the couch watching television. The teatime clock was ticking as light through the windows thinned and paled. The room began to cool. Gram would fire up the kettle before long; the card playing would soon come to a close. I could tell by the crescendo of voices, their animation, the slaps of palm to table. I could hear it in the laughter and the bursts of dismay or triumph: someone would soon be declared the winner.

Play yer cards close to yer belly button! Gramma would say. Though Ukko won the final round of bidding, it was clear by his grumbles he didn't really want it. He must have been "bidding her up," a tactic I'd seen used many times. "I'm goin' in the hole," he said.

Gram was laughing. "Bid high and sleep in the alley!"

Ukko shook his head. "One card! I just needed one damn card and I woulda had it."

Thanks to Gram's competitive spirit, I came to appreciate the whole feminist movement in a single afternoon.

Summer had come and gone as swift as a hummingbird. A day-long dump of snow had buried the drive beyond Gramma's porch, and it was still accumulating. She had told me and my sisters earlier we would need to shovel before dark. If we waited until morning, there would be more snow than we could handle, and we never knew when Uncle Andy, Gram's brother-in-law, would swing by with his plow to dig us out. In heavy snowfall, visitors parked along the roadside. All we had to do was shovel a narrow path to the highway so people could reach the porch steps.

Meanwhile, we sat around the kitchen table playing pinochle. I was seven years old and, after years of watching everyone else play, had finally been invited to join in. I learned in a very short time that the game was much harder to play than it looked. Behind us, the wood stove popped, and I could smell the sweet, tangy aroma of cream of tomato soup warming on a burner. I wasn't a tomato soup fan, but Gramma let me crush handfuls of saltines into my bowl, which made the red goop more tolerable. Sometimes she even splurged on oyster crackers, a true delicacy.

"Reka," Janie said. "You have to play a card. You're holding up the game."

"But whatever card I play, you'll take it." I had just played my last trump card and had no idea which card should lead next.

Anne shrugged. "That's how the game goes." She was seated across from Jane, nearest the door—slouched on her tailbone at the edge of her chair, feet propped up on the corner of mine. "Sometimes you lose your cards."

"But then I lose the game."

"So?" Jane said. "That's what happens."

"But I *always* lose."

54

"Just play."

"Play a card," Anne said. "It doesn't matter which one. She's gonna take it. She'll take mine too. Here, watch." She leaned in out of turn and placed a face card on the table. Janie slapped a trump card down over it. "See. She's got a good hand. We can't beat her."

"Maybe she's cheating." I bent down and looked under the table to see if I could catch her in the act.

"I'm not cheating!"

"What's goin' on in there?" Gram asked. She was sitting in the front room listening.

"Theresa won't play a card," Jane said. In Gram's house, I was "Theresa" when I was in trouble. "She's holding up the game."

"She takes all my cards!"

Grunting, Gramma hoisted herself off the couch and ambled into the kitchen. She stood beside me and bent in close to my ear. I smelled the smokey void of her mouth, a soothing constant. "Let's see what ya got," she said. I held my hand up, eyeing my sisters to make sure they didn't peek.

"Hearts is trump," Anne said.

Gram studied the cards clutched in my fingers and pulled one, raising it slightly above the rest. "Play that one."

"But…" I flashed her a panicked look and pointed to Janie's trump card lying on the table. I didn't see how Gramma's suggestion would prove helpful. Jane's card would beat it. That much I did know.

"It's okay." She gave me a nod. "Play it."

Reluctantly, I laid the card down on top of the other two. Janie swept all three cards across the table into her enviable pile, her trump card all-powerful. I looked to Gramma, my mouth agape. "See!"

"You win some, you lose some," she said. "But you gotta play the hand you're dealt."

FLINT SPARKS AN INTEREST

We were on our way to Houghton when I first saw him. I was pressed against the rear passenger-side door, my face an inch from the bottom of the window, breath fogging the cool glass in faint bursts. My older sisters were sitting up straight and proper, whispering to one another. I was rarely privy to their tête-à-têtes.

"There's ol' Flint," Mom said. "On his way back home."

We had just bounced over the diagonal railroad tracks signaling town was only a few miles ahead when we passed him. He was walking along the gravelly roadside. Given his posture and ship-shape appearance, you might have mistaken him for a soldier on his way to duty, except he was too old to qualify. His legs made up the biggest part of him. They were long and thin, draped in creased and pressed trousers which broke neatly at the laced tops of glossy oxfords. His arms jackknifed from his pants pockets. He was slender, with square shoulders and a straight back, sporting a hip-length gray jacket tidily zipped up the front.

A modest brown fedora, banded with what looked like a hair ribbon, perched smartly upon his well-groomed head. There was a jauntiness to his step. The sight puzzled me: a man walking this far from town, dressed for church.

"He walks everywhere," Mom said, mostly to herself.

I had no idea who Flint was, but it didn't surprise me that Mom did. Everybody knew everybody in the Copper Country. I was just too young to have met them all. The breath of my sisters warmed my back as their whispers ebbed, and they looked over my shoulder in his direction. Disinterested, they returned to their meeting of the minds.

The Mason house was a hubbub of activity as orange sunlight puddled behind Johnson's and the bats commenced their game of musical chairs amidst the trees. A scratchy record undulated on the turntable, and the TV screen flashed muted images in black and white. We rarely had the TV *and* the record player going at the same time. Earlier, Gramma had washed her hair over the kitchen sink with the White Rain shampoo she kept on top of the cabinet and wrapped her bangs in pink sponge rollers. Now, happy hips swung her from room to room as she unfurled her curls and sang a Dinah Shore song about the virtues of men.

It had been announced earlier that Gramma had a date. With Flint.

"Who will take care of us?" I asked.

"He's coming here," Gram said. "I'm not going anywhere."

"You have to be good," my sisters told me. "And go to bed when we tell you." There were pros and cons to having multiple mothers.

I was confused by this new development. It was scary to me—Gramma having a date with the man we had passed on the roadside. Where had they met? Gramma never left the house anymore, not even to go to the outhouse. When Mom had dated before she married Derry, it had seemed natural enough, but the idea of Gramma dating felt bizarre. What would happen to us? Would she get married too? In contrast to my inner turmoil, Gram seemed blithely happy about the event that was to occur right there in the Mason house with us girls as chaperones. I had no say in the matter.

From the closet in Aunty Patsy's old room, Gram retrieved a small cardboard box filled with a jumble of cosmetics, samples mostly, probably from Avon. We all joined her on the couch. Katie was there too that night. Fifty fingers rifled through cream sachets, miniature compacts, innumerable white plastic lipstick testers, and a talcum tin or two. Noses sniffed and rounded lips oohed and aahed at the bright colors and floral scents.

Gram rubbed a smear of rosy rouge onto her cheeks. She wiped an arc of red across her receding lips. Her favorite perfume, Evening in Paris, was delicately dabbed at the notch of her neck and behind each ear.

"Am I snazzy enough?" she asked, and winked.

To me, she was as beautiful as the NBC peacock, which I had seen *in living color* on my cousin's television. Her hair shone, and her bangs corkscrewed at her temples. I had never seen her this way. I wasn't sure what to make of it.

Gramma had a boyfriend.

Flint and Gram must have gotten along well on that date and the dates that followed, because one day I arrived at the Mason house to find him living in Aunty Patsy's old room. He had vacated his prior residence west of Mason, from which he had regularly walked the five miles there *and* back for his visits with Gramma.

With this new occupant, the Mason house shrunk. We weren't allowed to go upstairs anymore. That was *his* space now.

"He's like a boarder," Gram explained. "He's renting the room from me." Gram's parents had kept a boarding house when she was young, and she had told me stories of having to cook and clean for the men who lived there. Would we have to do the same for Flint? The prospect set me off in a silent tizzy.

Weeks passed, perhaps even months. I learned very little about Gram's relationship with Flint. She was oddly reserved about the whole situation. "Where did you meet him?" I asked one day, my curiosity getting the better of me.

"I used to know him," Gram said, a dreamy look in her eyes. "Long time ago." She didn't offer any further details.

Whether he was living there as a boarder or a boyfriend, I couldn't say, but as time went on I was glad his presence didn't affect the Mason house *too* much. As a matter of fact, Flint's presence in the room upstairs didn't seem to have too much effect on Gramma, either. When we arrived for our usual stays, he was usually nowhere to be seen. We rarely even heard the floor creak overhead. He kept the bedroom door closed much of the time, which blocked the afternoon sunlight from the stairwell, leaving it stark and foreboding. The only time I noticed him was when he came downstairs whistling, preparing for his daily walks, which went on rain or shine from what I recall. He always dressed like a church-goer and spoke very little to me, offering only a tepid smile, a quick wink, and a nod of his fedoraed head. Gramma didn't talk much about him until the day he took Jet-Jobber, who was still with us at the time, for a walk.

I bounded through the shed that day to find the dog lying on the big mat in front of the kitchen door. He barely moved when I entered. I reached down to pet him. "What's the matter with Jet-Jobber?" I asked. He was old, but he usually at least wagged his tail when he saw me.

Gram pressed her lips tight and pumped her thumb toward the ceiling. "Poor dog's wiped out," she said. She raised her chin with a jerk. "*He* took him for a walk down the tracks. They were gone forever. Jet-Jobber can't walk that far anymore. He's too old for that."

61

I didn't know what to say. Gram was clearly angry. The dreamy look had faded.

It was a sunny afternoon when Janie and I arrived in Mason for the weekend. Gram was in a sour mood again. This was happening more and more. I went to set my things down in Grampa's old room, where we slept since Flint's arrival. I returned to Gramma, where she sat stewing on the couch. Janie was still in the bedroom.

"*That* one'll be gone before long," she said, thumbing toward the ceiling in what, in recent weeks, had become a common gesture.

"Who? Flint?" I asked, a bit too loudly perhaps.

She flashed me a glance, index finger to her lips, then cupped her ears with her palms. I knew the signals: Be quiet. Big ears. Gram would have made a good umpire.

Not long after that brief exchange, I waltzed in on a Friday to find Gram's mood had changed. The clouds that had gathered over the house in recent weeks had lifted. No words were spoken about the situation upstairs, but I noticed the door to Aunty Patsy's room was wide open, the stairwell filled with light.

Flint had moved on.

Gramma never spoke again about Flint. At least not to me, anyway. After his quiet departure, space in the Mason house expanded by an entire floor, though we rarely went upstairs anymore except to hang clothes in the attic or dig through souvenirs. It turned out life could be lived comfortably within the four rooms of the first floor (plus, of course, the shed and the shit house).

For me, the memory of Gram's boarder faded quickly but not completely. The experience had widened my world. Once in a while, when I tagged along with Mom or Dad on trips to Houghton or Hancock, I was reminded of the dapper gentleman who'd once lived in Aunty Patsy's old room at the top of the steps. Sometimes, as I pressed my nose against the rear passenger window, I'd see a familiar figure walking along the roadside. *Look!* I'd say. *There's Flint!* I'd sit up on my knees and wave wildly, flashing a jack-o'-lantern grin as we passed.

He never took his hands out of his pockets. He'd just nod his fedoraed head.

TUTANKHAMEN

I was raised in a family of five siblings, but I was born into a family of seven. My two older brothers didn't survive.

My real dad was still living and Anne and Janie were toddlers when Mom learned she was pregnant with her third child. It was the late fifties, and Catholics tended to have their children close together—not always out of preference. Mom readied the nursery, carried the child to full term, and went into labor naturally, just as she had with her two previous births. Everything appeared fine.

But something had gone wrong long before they wheeled her into the delivery room. As her pain subsided, Mom heard the smack of a palm to a backside. There were rumblings of concern amongst the doctor and nurses. "He's not breathing."

"What's the matter with the baby?" Mom asked when she didn't hear him crying.

"We're just cleaning him up," the nurse lied.

It was some time before Mom learned he was gone. He was fully developed on the outside, but inside he was missing a lung. His intestines had migrated into the cavity the lung was supposed to inhabit. Mom's blood had nourished him and provided the oxygen his body needed to grow, but he could not survive untethered. When the umbilical cord was clipped, his life ended.

"I'll take care of everything," Aunty Jean assured Mom afterward. Aunty Jean was Gramma's oldest daughter. She and Mom had grown very close when Jean was widowed at a young age and moved back to the UP, pregnant with her first child. "I don't want you to have to worry about a thing. I'll arrange for the burial. I'll take care of all the details."

Mom never saw her baby. She left the hospital empty-armed. She had two toddlers at home who needed her. There was no time to mourn. "I had everything ready," she said years later, memories washing back. "It was weird going home without a baby. Sad." It seemed the revelation was freshly dawning, like she had finally earned the time to reflect.

Gram was the one who first told me about the poor baby, my oldest brother. He was known as Baby Boy Bertineau. I had come along four years later.

"Your dad saw that baby and down he went," Gram said with a chop to her palm. "White as a sheet." I thought the baby must have been visibly deformed. I thought it must have been so frightening a sight that my father keeled over in fear. But I was wrong.

"He was a normal, fully developed baby," Mom revealed once I'd become an adult. "That's what the hospital told me."

I don't know much about my father, but I know how he grieved the loss of his first son.

It was 1960 when Mom carried her fourth-born child home with her from the hospital. His name was Steven John. He was her second boy. The first son she would raise. By all accounts he was a sweet and silly boy. Gentle and inquisitive. Loving and affectionate. He was the only surviving male child in a patriarchal household, growing up a prince.

It was four years before Mom noticed something amiss.

"He wasn't gaining any weight," she said. "He wasn't playing anymore—wasn't peppy."

She took him to the doctor's office. They couldn't find anything to treat, so they told her to keep an eye on him. She did. Several months passed before she noticed a new symptom. "He'd started losing weight," she recalled. "His clothes were hanging on him." The doctor still had no answers.

In the first week of September, Stevie started kindergarten at the school in Dollar Bay, a few miles away. One morning he came downstairs. "Mama," he said. "I can't go to school. I'm too sick."

Mom didn't know what to make of it. He seemed okay, so she sent him on to school. By ten o'clock the school nurse was pulling up outside the house. She had brought Stevie home: He was running a high fever. Mom couldn't drive, so she called for a ride and brought him to the doctor that day.

"He's got rheumatic fever," the doctor informed her. They sent her home with a course of treatment. She laid cool cloths on his body to bring his temperature down.

His condition didn't improve.

She loaded him into our car the next morning and my father drove them to St. Joseph's Hospital in Hancock. As she was helping Stevie through the doors of the hospital, he suddenly crumpled into her arms like a tumbling tower of Jenga blocks. That was the last time he walked.

"They did all kinds of tests," she said years later. "Finally, Dr. Bonderz said they were gonna do a spinal tap. Sure enough, they found it there."

The doctor called her into a room. He said her son was dying. He had cancer. There was nothing they could do. Like my father upon his first son's death, Mom now collapsed. "Mrs. Bertineau, you have to be strong for that little boy," the doctor told her. "You have to go in there with a smile."

For three months, every day, Mom followed the doctor's orders. She entered Stevie's hospital room smiling, cheeks cemented, tears locked down. She spent her days there in that room while Gramma helped care for us girls. She didn't see our father much. Perhaps work kept him away. Or perhaps the loss of another son was more than he could bear.

"When am I gonna go home, Mama?" Stevie asked.

"Pretty soon," Mom said. "You'll get to go home pretty soon." By this time Stevie's stomach was distended with Wilms' tumor. His eyelashes had fallen out, his nails dropped off.

It was nearly Christmas when he died of nephroblastoma, a cancer of the kidney that generally afflicts children and eventually overtook my brother's spine. I was not yet three when he died; I don't remember him at all. I think we only had one photo of him: standing behind the rental house in Tamarack amongst a group of neighborhood kids, Anne and Janie beside him. They were wearing wet bathing suits, their hair limp and dripping. He was a darling little boy with dark hair, dark eyes, and mocha skin. A precious Chippewa boy.

It was a steamy summer day when Janie and I climbed the dark, narrow risers to the attic of our home. Heat hovered in the tight stairwell, snuffing out our breath like a pillow over our faces. She heaved open the overhead hatch, which was made of solid oak planks painted milky brown. The hinges ticked and wood creaked as she propped it against exposed studs that were aged to the color of tamarack bark. Light from the attic windows, one at each gable, streamed in through the dust. We didn't go up there often, but we were looking for something on this particular day—some insignificant item buried amidst steamer trunks, a gilded bird cage, and cartons of Christmas decor. I don't recall what it was.

I rummaged through a box that sat near the steps, lid propped open, cardboard decaying. Inside I uncovered a transparent bag, cinched at the top with a bread tie. It was filled with dozens of plastic miniatures, the kind of trinkets you get when you drop a penny into a gumball machine.

There was a stack of comic books too, *Archie* mostly, neatly pressed within plastic sleeves.

"Ooh," I said to Janie. "What's this?" The items were delicately preserved, like the treasures of Tutankhamen. Instinctively I knew not to disturb them.

"Don't touch those," Janie said. "Those are Stevie's. From the hospital."

She didn't say the things *were* Stevie's. She said they *are* Stevie's. They still belonged to him.

Somehow, he still belonged to us.

BIGMOUTH

Perhaps it was my youth, or perhaps my innate curiosity: I always wanted to be in the know. My problem was that once I *was* in the know, I didn't mind telling everyone else what I knew. That's how, at home, I came to be called Bigmouth—particularly when it involved my two older sisters. If I overheard them talking about something, I was always sure to pass it along.

"Anne needs Kotex," I announced one morning at the breakfast table. I'd heard her bemoaning the fact at the top of the stairs in Grandma Nelson's part of the house. I'd gone in to get my mittens where they were drying on top of the yellow radiator. My sisters' voices carried. Sometimes I could hear them fighting over shoes before school.

"Hey, hey, hey!" Dad said, waving his hand in my direction. "We don't need to talk about that stuff at the table." He wore a shit-eatin' grin on his face—at least, that's what he would have called it. Dad had a good sense of humor when he wasn't worrying about money.

"How do you know about *that*?" Mom asked, alarmed by my newly acquired knowledge. She kept the Kotex hidden away at the back of the bottom shelf in the bathroom. I had seen them there in a big flowered box, and the little white belts that went with them.

"I heard her say it. She's gonna have to ask Dad to get some at the IGA when she comes downstairs."

"Don't be a big mouth," Mom said. "And quit talking about it now." Period talk was taboo.

My sisters had their own rooms in Grandma Nelson's section of the house, which was connected to our rambler addition by what used to be the back porch—an alcove that now served as a laundry room and bathroom. Grandma Nelson's house was a tall, narrow two-story high above the abandoned Calumet & Hecla smelter site on the shores of Torch Lake. C&H was the granddaddy of the mining companies, even bigger than Quincy. Grandma Nelson's husband had worked for C&H in their reclamation plant, chemically separating copper from stamp sands. He'd died there as well. She told me about it once. She said someone ran up to the house to tell her something had happened.

"He went to work feeling just fine," she said. "He had his coffee..." Her voice trailed off. "Something burst." An aortic aneurysm had ended his life that day. She poked at her abdomen with her thumb and three fingers as she tried to recall the medical term, but the words eluded her. She smacked her tongue, pursed her mauve lips, and looked off in the direction of the smelter far beyond her living room window. "Yah," she said, concluding the discussion. I was expected to understand, and somehow I did.

Grandma Nelson's home was bright, with lots of windows, three bedrooms, an eat-in kitchen, and a formal dining room. All her furnishings matched, even her dishes. I was unaccustomed to such fixtures. I think most everything we owned had been handed down or came from the Jewel Tea man. On her front porch, a wooden shingle with the name "Nelson" swung from two small chains. This was the home my stepdad had been raised in.

After Mom and we four girls moved in, the house took on a whole new life. It went from the two of them—Dad and Grandma Nelson—to the seven of us. Grandma Nelson didn't seem too pleased with the arrangement. Within a couple of years, the number rose to eight with the birth of my half brother Chris. When he came along, Katie lost her bedroom. She had to move into mine. I wasn't happy about that at all. Dad bought us bunk beds, though, to make up for the situation. I'd seen bunk beds on *The Brady Bunch*, so the fact that *we* had them made me feel special. I didn't know of many stepchildren. Especially stepchildren with bunk beds like the Bradys.

Sometimes, amidst the chaos, I would go upstairs to visit with my sisters. It was quiet up there—a nice place to take a break. Janie had moved into our stepaunt's old bedroom. It was a spacious room with carnation pink walls and a window overlooking our cousins' house next door. Anne slept in Dad's old room. They painted it lavender for her, a very soothing shade. There were honey-hued hardwood floors and porcelain doorknobs as dark as onyx, smooth and round as beach stone. The closet in Anne's room held the steps to the attic, which used to scare me when she let me sleep with her on occasion. I was afraid of attics.

Anne's room was also the furthest room from the rambler—a safe space. Sometimes, if we could reach it, we hid there when violence broke out downstairs. Mom and Dad were drinking more and more. Beer was ruining everything. At times, the rambler could become like the attic—a scary place. Upstairs, we still heard what went on below, but Grandma Nelson must not have. She never came out of her bedroom, which was probably for the best given she was fragile as a crackled Christmas bulb—one tumble and we'd be sweeping up the pieces. It was okay, though; in Anne's room we kids felt far enough removed from the peril—like it wasn't really happening to us, like some unknown neighbors were suffering instead. I always felt sorry for them—whoever they were. If we younger ones couldn't get upstairs, Anne and Janie found a way to get to us, to slip through the mayhem, risking their own safety. Sometimes it took a while, but eventually the door to our bedroom would slowly open. They would slip silently inside, Chris in their arms, and secure the door behind them. We'd all wait it out together, huddled on the lower bunk in the bedroom Katie and I shared. Then it was us I felt sorry for.

This family secret was something we dared not share with anyone; even with my blabber mouth, I had never spoken of it to another soul. It was one reason I loved being with Gramma in Mason. Her home was a lot like Anne's room—safe and soothing.

It was late afternoon. The sun spilled in from the west through the window behind the birdcage in the Mason house. Rays fell soft and golden upon Gramma's face where she sat beside my sisters in her sunken spot at the end of the couch, a quart of Pabst and a half-filled glass on the table beside her. I could see the folds of her brow and the perpetual downward arc of her lips. Her fleshy eyelids, like bread dough, rested heavy atop short lashes. Thin cheeks caved inward around her long nose. She was a dishwater blonde and wore her hair cropped at the chin and bridged by severe bangs, which she trimmed to squarely frame her face.

"They fight a lot now," Anne said of our parents. "I worry about the kids."

Anne didn't consider herself a kid anymore. She was fourteen and had already lived through a lot. She was old enough to have vivid memories of our real dad and rebellious enough to resent the new one. She remembered our brother Stevie well and had lived through his death alongside my mother and father. Stevie had died just a year before our real dad, and Mom still struggled to talk about him, except after dark, if she'd been drinking. Sometimes I'd awaken in the night to hear her anguished laments of him beyond my bedroom door. In Hubbell, I learned that when Dad drank, he'd rant about President Nixon, but when Mom drank, she'd rage at God.

When Anne talked about "the kids," it was me and my younger sister and brother. She and Jane, who was closest to her in age, were growing up too fast. They'd been groomed by stress and saddled with the role of emergency caretakers to us younger ones. The drinking at home had its demands. My sisters weren't as carefree as some of their friends—I saw it in them. I saw the difference when they brought their friends around. My sisters were more responsible with us, always alert. That stirred guilt in me—there was a lot of guilt in the Hubbell house—yet I was grateful too. I depended on them.

I watched them as they sat on the midnight-blue upholstery with the flocked brocade. It had frayed over the years, and curly strands of straw-like batting erupted from beneath, like a tattered bird's nest. I lay across from them on my back in the matching chair with its big, rolled arms. My legs were propped against the curved seat back, head dangling off the cushion, hair sweeping the floor. We could sit like that in the Mason house. Gram didn't care.

Up until this day, my sisters and I had spoken only to each other of the torment at home, the violence. To hear something said aloud to Gramma was alarming. What if Mom and Dad found out? We'd be in big trouble. Gramma might get in trouble too. I sure didn't want that to happen. There were enough problems between my parents and her as it was. Once, after Gram and Dad had a tiff, he didn't let us see her for weeks. I couldn't imagine what he'd do if he knew about this.

"And in the morning, we still have to go to school," Janie said. "We have to get the kids up and make sure we don't miss the bus."

"And everything's a mess," Anne said.

"We clean up what we can," Janie added.

This was true. In the past, I'd heard the *chink* of broken glass as it slid from our copper dustpan into the trashcan—dishes that had met their deafening demise in the night. I'd heard the thud of chairs being uprighted in the kitchen and the table being slid back into place. I'd also heard it all come undone the night before, of course: chairs flying, table plowing, thunder in the drywall. The furor rattled our bedroom door as I lay in my bunk, bones bouncing, teeth clacking. Fear's captive. Monsters warred in the kitchen, yet I was too afraid to run, too afraid to move. I learned to ignore my instincts, to melt into the mattress, make my breath shallow, sink deep beneath my pilled, floral blanket with the silky blue trim, the one Dad and Mom had received as a wedding gift. I lay waiting—maybe for rescue, maybe for something else.

Mornings after, while my sisters tampered with evidence, they would whisper and tiptoe about. When the coast was clear, only then would they lead us to the bathroom in the tiny alcove between Grandma Nelson's and the rambler. *Maybe they won't drink again for awhile*, we would tell each other. There was always hope. We'd learned that at St.

Cecilia's in Hubbell where Mom took us to church, though she didn't seem to like it much there anymore.

"And no one can sleep," Anne said.

"Until they do." Janie was like an extension of Anne. She could finish her sentences, clarify ambiguities. She was prim and proper, right and just—almost to a fault. In some ways, she was the inverse of my oldest sister, though they were thick as thieves. Where Anne was lanky, Jane was stout. While Anne's expressions were prone to be sober, Janie's smile could melt every heart in the room. Her duteous nature was the ballast to Anne's streak of mischief. It was as if Mary Poppins and Pippi Longstocking had joined forces.

The conversation went on; Gramma listened, somber and silent. I lay still, observing them upside down. Despite my fears, there was a freedom in speaking our secret. The weight of it lightened. The words dredged up the shame from rock bottom, except that in the light I could see it wasn't really *us* who should be ashamed—it was Dad and Mom. Why were *we* carrying all that around, trying to act normal? Other kids didn't seem to have these problems. I was sure Mom and Dad weren't supposed to act this way. Something welled up inside me then, a grown-up sort of strength and indignation. There was more, too—a dark, insidious, beastly thing—hatred. In catechism, Father Cole had taught us that hatred was wrong, but in this instance I couldn't help myself. I hated beer. I hated its rancid, yeasty smell. I hated being afraid to fall asleep, wondering if it was safe, listening for signs. I'd wait for the pop of a top or the clink of a bottle to a glass. Sometimes, if I was still up, I'd make jokes and tell funny stories, hoping humor could trump beer like in pinochle. I'd try to distract Mom and Dad, but I couldn't. No matter what I did, they drank anyway.

Through the years I'd adhered to the rule of secrecy where this topic was concerned, but the gates had swung open now. My belly roiled; my throat burned. I bolted upright in my chair and spewed like an angry pop bottle. "And then *you* drink!" I spat. Gramma looked at me with a start. I was crossing some invisible line—that line between child and adult—but I couldn't keep it inside. "Our parents drink and fight, and then we come here, and all you do is drink too!"

As soon as the words were out I regretted them. Gramma's face crumpled. Her eyes brimmed with tears, like glistening beads of mercury—poison to me. My sisters' mouths gaped, and Anne shot me an if-looks-could-kill glare. It was clear I'd committed a wrong—I'd hurt Gramma. I had never done that before, had never wanted to. I just needed to be heard. Could I have taken the words back, I would have done so in a flash. I would have gulped them back down, buried them like mothballs in the attic, but it was too late. Some secrets were best kept hidden. *Words can wound*, I'd heard people say.

Would I ever learn to keep my big mouth shut?

TEARS AT TEATIME

Though Gram preferred beer after five o'clock, tea was her brew of choice earlier in the day. No matter the season, not a day passed when the teakettle failed to whistle. Though I knew how much she enjoyed her tea, I didn't appreciate its true value until one particular summer stay when I was perhaps eight years old.

I had been in Mason for some time, and the grocery sack that served as my suitcase was empty except for one white anklet with no mate. Gram washed out all my things in the kitchen sink and together we climbed the steep steps to the attic, where there was a clothesline strung across the dark, narrow expanse at the back of the house.

I squatted near her, digging through a shallow box of dusty keepsakes while she hung my shorts, shirts, and underpants with turquoise-colored clothespins. "Hey," I said. "Who's this?" I had uncovered a large black-and-white photo of two older men standing on a porch. I couldn't tell if it was Gramma's porch or not, though the architecture was similar. Both men were wearing suit coats and looked distinguished.

"Oh. That's your Grampa and…" She paused and looked closer, snapping her thumb and middle finger together briskly. She had been trying to teach me to snap like that, but my version still sounded more like a *splat*. "It's right on the tip of my tongue."

I studied the photo too. "Grampa" wasn't Grampa Bertineau, her husband. It was Great-Grampa Otten. He looked so young in the photo, his hair salt and pepper instead of the bright white I remembered, his skin taut.

"Cripes, I can't think of it now." Gram clipped the last pieces of clothing onto the line and moved toward the door. "You want that picture?"

"Yeah! Can I?"

"Grab it and let's get going. It's hot as hell up here. I'm wringin' wet." She pulled the string on the ceiling light and shut the door behind us, leaving my clothes to drip-dry in the smothering heat beneath the rafters. "I need my cup of *tay*," she said. Sometimes she pronounced it that way.

"Won't tea make you hotter?"

"Nah. Tea's good for everything."

Sun flooded Grampa's old bedroom, where Gram and I slept all the time now. The enameled aqua walls gleamed, gold-plated and fervent. She was already up and about. I could hear her loafers clopping about in the kitchen while she chatted with Pretty Bird, her canary. "I tawt I taw a puddy tat," she said.

There was something about sunny days and that yellow bird. They seemed parts of the same whole—bright, cheerful, beckoning. I lay there, swaddled by the sounds of the house, wondering if it was like this even when I wasn't here. Was it this happy? Did it feel this good? I wished I could stay at the Mason house forever, though I never told anyone that. I didn't think kids should want to live with anyone other than their own Mom and Dad.

In the kitchen, the window was open to the world, propped up on its screen. Outside I could hear the babel of birds in the scraggly mulberry tree and the persistent buzz of houseflies seeking a way indoors. I ate a bowl of Corn Flakes at the table, milk dribbling down my chin. Gramma sashayed about the house with her wide hips swinging.

"It looks pretty out today," I said, smacking between spoonfuls.

"Yup," she said. "How sweet it is!" Jackie Gleason sayings were part of Gram's repertoire. She was scavenging through the pantry closet. "I think we're gonna do some cleaning today."

Cleaning day? Yes! Cleaning day was so much fun. If I were lucky, she would dig out all the old stuff and show it to me again: the scary coin bank, her new sweaters that she'd never taken out of the plastic, Grampa Bertineau's war stuff.

Before I could finish getting dressed, she had deployed the record player in the front room. It was a GE Wildcat with a beige plastic shell and a handle on the top. It sat like a suitcase on the parlor table until you flipped the front down.

She kept a stack of records on the shelf below—LPs, some 45s, and even a few 78s. A moment later, I heard the smack of an album on the turntable followed by static as the stylus skimmed the vinyl. A bluesy voice marked the pickup, and a bright burst of brass lit up the house. Ray Charles's red-covered country-and-western album would start us off with "Bye Bye Love."

Yes, it was most definitely going to be a great day!

In the kitchen, Gram whistled along with the record as she cleaned. I took the maroon, floppy-headed dust mop from a hook in the shed and worked my way from room to room, dusting under and around the furniture. Gramma didn't like to dust anymore—she said she had a touch of rheumatism. When the album had played through, she took requests. "Reka, what d'ya wanna hear next?" she called from the front room.

"Doggie in the window!"

I heard her flipping through the 45s in search of the little disc with the red Mercury label. I knew which records carried which labels—it made them easier to spot in the pile when I was allowed to stack them on the record changer. After a brief hiss of static, the soothing vocals of Patti Page brought me running to the front room. Gramma was already singing.

We stood beside the window, accompanying the record. At times, she'd break into a little bark just like the song, grinning, swaying. She loved music, and how contagious her passion! Beyond the window, the lush, lobed leaves of the sugar maple shimmied in the breeze, shading the front of the old house. Dapples of sunlight flickered through green clusters; I could almost hear the glints of light tinkling like chimes.

By early afternoon, the Wildcat was running hot, but the house was clean. As I'd hoped, we proceeded with our ritual of looking at all the memorabilia Gram kept tucked away. It began downstairs, where she retrieved the coin bank from the metal wardrobe and sat with me on the bed. It was a simple black cube, but inside nested a ghoulish hand that rose industrially and snatched a coin from a slot.

"Let's see if still works," she said. She opened a small door on the bottom of the bank and removed one of a few pennies. In some homes one might find pennies buried in seat cushions, but in the Mason house the copper discs were a precious commodity. She glanced at me with mischief in her eyes. "Don't get too close." Gears ground as the hand reached out to grasp the coin and then disappeared within. I giggled. She grinned.

In the spare room upstairs, we sifted through the old bureau with the brass-ring pulls left smooth and burnished by the oils of family fingers. I saw a sweater we'd given her one year as a gift, still neatly wrapped in cellophane. There were dainty ladies' handkerchiefs, starched and crisply folded, one vibrant with purple and gold pansies. "You like that one, don't you, Gram?" I asked.

"Mm hmm. Pansies are always pretty. My favorite flower."

The big brown box below the north eave held the treasure trove of Grampa Bertineau. He had served in World War I and had been plagued by health issues ever afterward— perhaps from exposure to mustard gas, my uncle once said. Grampa was fifteen years older than Gram and had died of a cerebral hemorrhage in 1958, well before I was born. Gram rarely spoke of him, except when she opened the lid to this box.

Mom had told me that the two of them used to fight a lot when she lived in Mason. She'd be upstairs in her bedroom and would hear them yelling below all day long. It was clear to her that they didn't get along, although she once saw a different side to their relationship.

"He'd been away for awhile," Mom said. "The bus dropped him off out front, and your gramma was right there waiting for him. She was really happy to see him—huggin' him and kissin' on him. It was real cute." She chuckled. "That didn't last long, though. A few days later they were at it again."

Our Grampa came from a large French Canadian family. I'd heard he was handsome and built close to the ground, compact, with sturdy legs. He'd descended from voyageur stock—French Canadian fur trappers. They had to be built like that in order to have a good center of balance in the canoes; that's what my uncle said. Grampa came from a home where French was the primary language. I imagined he had passed some of that on to Gram, because once in a while she sang or spoke to me in French. *Comment allez-vous?* she'd say when we kissed her hello, or *Comment ça va?* like some war widow on the French fronts. I'd heard my grandparents were considered to be from opposite sides of the tracks. Not only were their ethnicities different, but also their families' religions—hers Protestant, his Catholic. I knew very little about him other than that. She never spoke of their marriage nor wore a wedding band. To me, she'd been a widow and a gramma all her life—she'd been one all *my* life at least, though my grampa's influence still presided over that house. It seeped from his fancy army portrait that hung near the oil stove in an ornate oval frame.

"This was part of his mess kit," Gram said. She had pulled up a chair alongside the box. She lifted a roll of drab canvas from within and gently unfolded it. Inside was cutlery: a spoon, a knife, and a fork. She let me hold them before carefully rolling them back up. There was a navy-blue handkerchief from his funeral; the billy club he'd carried in service. The club was dark and solid, with grooves carved in the grip. A thin, leather wrist strap was attached. There was a divot in the wood near the end of the club.

"Where'd that chip come from?" I asked.

"He probably knocked some bugger over the head," she said. The billy club was familiar to me, because it was always threatened as the answer to Gramma's problems. Whenever there was talk on Channel 6 of some seedy characters wreaking havoc in the Copper Country, Gramma would hold up her fist. *They better not come 'round here*, she'd say. *I'll get the bloody billy club after 'em.*

Our examination of the past complete, she tucked all Grampa's things back inside the box and stood up. She looked tired. "I think I'll go back down now. Why don't you play up here awhile? Till supper."

The spare room held a few toys—a miniature art deco kitchen set, an Etch A Sketch, and some blocks—so I agreed, but I didn't last long. The upstairs was spooky without her. I was afraid of the closets and the dark, menacing attic door looming at the top of the stairwell. Music played downstairs as the light in the room grew anemic and the shadows donned stilts. It was almost teatime. I descended the mottled treads of the steps, their surfaces worn smooth and concave. When I reached the landing, something caught my attention—a low and wheezy snuffle coming from the parlor, like a tailpipe buried in snow. I knew the Mason house inside and out. I knew the light through its windows at each time of day, the odors in its air; I especially knew its sounds. This one, however, was hard to identify. It was akin to Gramma's laughter—guttural and rhythmic, like when she had just heard a really good joke on *The Honeymooners* or gotten to laughing at her own imitations of Woody Woodpecker. I went around the kitchen side of the house—the Mason house was one continuous square—and paused near the wood stove. What was she doing? Was she on the phone? The sounds persisted, so I peeked around the corner. She was hunched over on the edge of the rocker, shoulders heaving, head hanging. Tears dotted the skirt of her housedress.

Our fun cleaning day had come to an end.

I'd seen Gram cry on several occasions, but it had been awhile. She waxed emotional at times, usually when she'd been drinking, though not always. She used to go on "crying jags," we called them. Sorrow overtook her and she would cry and cry inconsolably. Her losses were many—like Mom's—and sometimes, I think, she just needed to feel them.

One night, when I was very young, Gram set to crying while we all sat in the front room. "What happened to Gramma?" I asked my sisters. I was watching TV and had missed what brought it on.

"She's okay," Anne said. "It's just a crying jag."

"She'll get over it pretty soon," Janie said. The black-and-white TV flickered in the corner of the room. We girls stared at it numbly as we encircled her, patting her arms and rubbing her back. Eventually, her crying subsided and we all climbed the steps to bed. That was just the way she was.

Now, I approached her where she sat in the rocker and wrapped my arm around her shoulder. "What's wrong, Gramma?" From the living room I could hear Doris Day with Les Brown and His Orchestra. It was the 78 with the red label—a soldiers' favorite, "Sentimental Journey." That song could make a clown cry. Gram shook her head and patted my hand with her damp one. The sobs had robbed her of her voice. Not knowing what to do, I left to get some tissues from the box on the back of the couch. I placed them in her palm when I returned and perched beside her on the wooden arm of the chair. "Is it this record?" I asked. "Too sad?" She couldn't answer, so we sat until her sobs ebbed. The record had finished playing; I could hear the needle rubbing against the label.

Finally, she spoke. "Gramma's okay, honey." She dabbed the end of her pointed Otten nose with the wad of cotton. "Thank you for the tissues." I didn't know what more I could do. I wanted to make everything better—to take away her pain—but I didn't know how. Had my sisters been there, they would have known. She took a deep breath, straightened herself, and looked up at me. "Can you fix Gramma a big cup o' tea?"

Of course. Why hadn't I thought of that? Tea was good for everything.

RESCUED: IN RETROSPECT

Despite its occasional storms of melancholy, the Mason house was a refuge for me. It was a safe, quiet place where I could regroup and recharge—my sanctuary. But it wasn't that way for everyone who crossed its threshold. It wasn't that way for Mom when she first came to live there.

It was the late forties when Mom's path began to carry her in the direction of the Mason house. That was when she first caught sight of my real dad. She said it scared her when she saw him riding through L'Anse with some buddies—a new white boy in a reservation town. (Of course there were other white boys in that blended community, but she'd seen them all before.) The car had *ML* plates—a Houghton County vehicle. Her older friends chased along after it. "ML plates! ML plates!" they squealed. They liked Houghton County boys. The car stopped and he climbed out, long legs and all. Mom's girlfriends gushed as though David Nelson himself had just stepped out of *The Adventures of Ozzie and Harriet* from the radio. Mom said Dad was a nice-looking boy; he must have been used to the attention.

"C'mon over!" Mom's girlfriends called to her. "Come talk to him!"

My dad called to her too. "Hey! You in the red jacket!"

"I didn't go anywhere near 'em," Mom said. "I was too scared." She was only eleven years old and didn't talk to strangers. "I was just a shy Indian girl from the sticks!" she said, laughing.

Fortunately for me, that would not be their last encounter.

"I saw him again a year or so later," Mom said. "He started coming around. He was driving by this time." She'd see him cruising through L'Anse, hanging out with his friends. They talked cars. He liked cars. "He seemed friendly enough." she said. "And I was a little older by then, so I wasn't so scared to talk to him."

It was the early fifties when Mom's home life began to unravel. By this time, her parents' drinking had settled in, heavy as a soaked hide. It drew a lot of trouble to their property, especially at night. Crowds gathered, lit by booze, senses askew, hooting and hollering till the wee hours of the morning. Sometimes Mom took her brothers and ran—into the woods or up the road to a friend's. Sometimes she went alone.

Fearing for her safety and the safety of her brothers, she began to tell others what was going on. She wanted help.

"I wasn't safe in that house anymore," she said. "Your dad would sometimes come and get me. He'd watch out for me." She didn't need David Nelson to idolize; she had my father. She fell in love with him, her protector. There were four years between them—five, if you counted the two days between their birthdays. But it appeared neither of them was counting.

"I was fifteen when it happened," Mom said. "When the county finally stepped in and took us away. What a mess. We were the talk of the town, I tell ya."

My father was hauled in too. He was considered an adult now, and the age difference between Mom and him created a big problem. The county wanted to straighten everything out at once. In the meantime, all the adults had to sit in jail, including my father.

Mom became a ward of the ominous St. Joseph's Orphanage in Assinins, a tiny village on the western banks of Keweenaw Bay. She'd been aware of the place in the past but had managed to avoid going near it. Now, she was a captive of the red-brick citadel that loomed high on a hillside offering a deceptively picturesque view of the waters of Lake Superior. She said that after that, she didn't see my father for weeks. As a matter of fact, she didn't see any visitors.

"I don't remember much about it," Mom said. "I just know I was in there. And you had to work hard. I remember scrubbing the steps. I didn't do it the way they wanted, and the nun hit me across my arm with a strap." She thought some more. "You had to do everything *just* the way they wanted it. You could never relax in there. Someone was always watching you. And they were *mean*. In other rooms, I heard kids screamin' and cryin'…. It was scary."

She and her brothers were separated at the orphanage. It was hardest on my Uncle Ray. He was just a little boy at the time and very attached to Mom. "I wasn't allowed to see them," she said. "Boys and girls were kept in separate blocks. The only time I got to see 'em was in the dining hall. I remember one time…Ray saw me…ran over to me. Oh, he was crying. 'I wanna go home, Sis!' he cried. 'I don't like it here!'" Mom paused as the memory surfaced. It gasped for air. It had been a long while since she'd let it breathe.

She continued. "There was nothing *I* could do. The nuns wouldn't let me. I tried to comfort him in the little time I had. 'Ma'll come and get us,' I told him before they took him away. I knew we were only supposed to be in there for six weeks. I told him, 'Not much longer. Just hang on now.'"

She was right. In time, they were released to their mother, who had served her time for the neglect of her children. Their father was still incarcerated. It would be some time before he returned to the family. "He was a nice man," Mom said in his defense. "We did have some good times. He was real gentle. He never yelled at us or hit us. But once he and my ma got started drinking, they didn't quit."

This I understood.

When they left the orphanage, life improved. Mom thought things were finally back on track. "Everything seemed good for about six months," she said. "Ma did real well. She didn't drink at all." But somewhere inside, her mother struggled. Perhaps she was lonely for her husband. Perhaps the draw of the wine was just too powerful. "One day I came home and she was drunk," Mom said. "And it started all over again, only worse. Ma blamed me for everything. She blamed me for my dad not being there. 'Look what you did!' she'd yell at me." There were times Mom couldn't even go home for fear of her mother's rage and abuse. "I didn't want to go back to that orphanage. I didn't know what to do."

My father was back in the picture now, trying to help again. A judge called them in. "He's my boyfriend," Mom explained that day in the courtroom. "He helps me. He keeps me safe when there's trouble at home."

"You're too young," the judge told her, but he understood the dilemma—sometimes girls grew up fast on the reservation. He looked at my father. "If you wanna take care of her, then you should marry her."

"I'll marry her," my father said. "She can live with me in Mason." He didn't want her to have to return to the orphanage. He wanted to protect her. He wanted to rescue her. He thought that was his role. But they'd have to wait a little while, until she turned sixteen. That was the youngest she could marry.

"I think that would be the best thing to do," the judge said.

It was the week of Mom's sixteenth birthday. She came home clutching a legal form. "Will you sign this?" she asked her ma, hands trembling. "I wanna get married."

"*En',*" her ma said in agreement, her first language slipping out. "I'll sign it." She wasn't in a mothering mood.

A day or so later, Mom dressed in a full, floral skirt cinched with a wide belt. Her skin looked warm as fresh coffee against her white blouse. She wanted to look nice for our father on their wedding day. She wanted to please her husband-to-be, who had turned twenty a few days before. He was a man now as he drove to collect her. He came to her door dressed in pleated trousers, a white button-down, and a long swing necktie in a geometric print. His father, my Grampa Bertineau, was with him. Gramma didn't want him to get married, so she'd stayed home in protest. She was headstrong that way. They all drove to the courthouse, where Mom and Dad were wed.

"After that," Mom said, "we ran by the house, picked up all my stuff, and off we went. I was fifteen one day and married the next." That day, she said goodbye to the reservation. She left her life behind. She left her little brothers too. "I was worried sick about them," she said. "But Blue was older then. I knew he'd watch over Ray. And Ma wasn't mad at them the way she was me."

She rode with her handsome new husband to Houghton County. He walked her inside his childhood home—the Mason house—the place where they would live with his parents as man and wife. That afternoon he showed her off to family and friends. She thought he was proud of her. She thought that, finally, all trouble was behind her. But it turned out she had landed in a fresh patch.

"Some girls knocked at the shed door that evening and off he went," she said of my dad. "I told him, 'Hey, you can't go off with them! You're married to me now.' But he just went, left me sitting at that house alone."

In the months that followed, his absence became a pattern. It would be some time before he settled into his new role, though eventually he did. Perhaps my father wasn't quite ready to be a man yet. Perhaps he wanted just a little more time to be the desirable boy.

"I just sat upstairs in that bedroom," Mom said. "Waiting." She didn't have any place else to go, and she loved him. "Downstairs I could hear your gramma and grampa fighting all the time. I didn't know what the heck I'd gotten myself into. They were always goin' at it." In those years, she said, Gramma was a bitter woman, and Grampa was in ill health. At times, they both drank too.

Mom began to wonder if she'd been rescued at all.

GIFTS OF GRACE

Even amidst dysfunction, magic can exist. Such was the case for our family. Despite the alcoholism and grief, there was still tradition, and part of that tradition—a part which to me was magical—was our unabashed celebration of the holidays.

It was nearly Christmas, 1971, and the only gift beneath Gramma's tree was a carton of Pall Malls. It was wrapped in holiday paper, but even a child could figure out what it was, since the one thing her gramma always wanted most at Christmas was cigarettes and that was what she usually got, year after year.

I stomped in through the shed in my snow boots, carrying my contribution to the sparse gift display. Earlier that week, Dad and Mom had given us each a small allotment of cash for Christmas shopping. One night after dark, Mom had driven us to Houghton, the metropolis just across the Portage. She had pulled up alongside the curb to let us out while she ran errands around town. "Watch your sister!" she had called to Janie from inside the car. "Hold her hand!"

I looked up at Janie that night as she grasped my mittened hand, her black hair glistening with snowflakes that appeared to sift down from the streetlights overhead. She was old enough to leave the house without a chook in the winter, but I had on my stocking cap with the spray of red yarn at its tip. We traipsed through the mountainous snowbanks between the parking meters, scurrying from storefront to storefront, but we struggled to find what we wanted.

"We're going to Newberry's," Janie finally declared. "That's the best."

Newberry's was to shoppers what the mother lode was to miners. It was vast and bright and sold most everything I'd ever seen in catalogs and on TV commercials. It was also cheap. She held the glass door for me as I slipped in beneath her arm. We crossed the boot-tracked, hollow-sounding floor to the women's section—a jungle of clothing racks, shoes, and carousels and tables adorned with costume jewelry.

"You'll find something here," she said with a quick, confident nod.

We milled about for a moment before settling on a three-foot square table teetering with small gift boxes. There were bracelets, screw-on earrings, necklaces, and fancy hairpins, each nestled in a square of white sponge. One stack held large brooches, which looked to me like something a grandmother would wear. I rummaged through the pile, opening the box tops and studying each piece with a discerning eye. Finally, it appeared. The perfect one. It was oval in shape with a white, porcelain-like background. On its face was printed an elaborate French woman, like Marie Antoinette, in a blue-gray costume with a dazzling plume of feathers billowing from her head. She looked sassy and elegant, like Gramma did when she washed her hair with White Rain shampoo. Adding to its pretentiousness was an antiqued metal setting, to which the glass oval had been shoddily affixed. I looked at the sign in the chrome stand above the table. It read "one dollar." That was exactly what I was allotted for Gramma's gift. Janie loaned me a few pennies for the tax, and my shopping was complete.

I now kicked off my boots in Gram's kitchen, gift in hand, and made a beeline to the Christmas tree in the far corner of the front room. It was an artificial pine about three feet tall, towering above the wooden parlor table where she normally kept the record player. That tree had always seemed a little sad to me. Dad harvested a real tree, fresh from the woods, for the Hubbell house. Gram didn't seem to mind her tree, though. The synthetic evergreen twinkled with small, multicolored lights, a glass topper, and a few silvery-brown bulbs with spiraled cutouts in their bellies painted red and green.

"I bought you a Christmas present!" I announced. I had never bought her a gift before. Mom and Dad must have encountered a windfall of some sort. I placed it next to the wrapped carton of cigarettes. "I picked it out all by myself!"

"Oh, honey. You didn't need to spend money on Gramma like that."

"They said I could. Mom took us to Houghton."

"Well, that was real nice. I'll have a very merry Christmas." She was sitting on the couch, and when I bent to kiss her hello she patted my side. "Be sure to thank your ma and dad for me too. Money's hard to come by these days."

It was midafternoon. *The Secret Storm* was on television. I didn't pay much attention to soap operas—too boring for me—but once in a while Gramma watched them, though she seemed to prefer game shows. The Christmas tree was still dark, awaiting dusk when we would plug it in.

"What do you want Santa to bring you?" she asked. *The Secret Storm* had ended and a string of toy commercials began.

"*You* know," I said, smiling. I had been telling her—and everyone else who would listen—how badly I wanted the new Malibu Barbie for Christmas. My cousin Lisa and I had both had that Barbie at the top of our lists since our first glimpse of the television commercial.

"I know," she said, grinning. "A Barbie doll."

"The *Malibu* Barbie. It has to be that one."

"Were you a good girl this year?"

"Yeah." I nodded. "I was good."

Or at least I'd tried to be.

On Christmas morning, my eyes popped open in my Hubbell bedroom, my gut flip-flopping with the joy and excitement of the day. Katie was already awake, glued to the bedroom door. The previous afternoon, that door had been fitted on the opposing side with a small hook-and-eye so we couldn't come out until our parents were up and the coffee ready. It was Dad who had devised the lock plot. I'd watched him screw the hardware into the jamb. He had fashioned the hook himself out of a small strip of copper he retrieved from Grandma Nelson's cellar. "What's that for?" I'd asked. His lips gripped a smoldering Doral, and the white stick see-sawed as he mumbled his answer. "To keep you two monkeys in your room until your ma and I are ready for ya." It seemed like an elaborate measure, but if there was one thing Dad and Mom didn't want to miss, it was the look on our faces when we first saw the tree on Christmas morning.

"Did Santa come?" Katie whispered, her eyes sparkling like tinsel, her hair amuck like a Wooly Willy.

"I hope so." I rolled onto my belly and slid over the edge of the top bunk until my toes skimmed the mattress below and sank down onto the cold floor. The rambler didn't have a cellar; it was set on a cement slab. "Are they up? Can you open the door?" Katie tried to pull the door open but met resistance. I went and gave it a good wiggle myself.

She pulled at the door again and called out through the tiny crack of light. "I need to go to the *baffroom*!" Her speech had improved through the years, but she still struggled with certain consonants.

From across the hall came Dad's voice. "Yah, yah. We hear ya." Despite the fact Christmas was his favorite time of year, he wasn't a morning person. Suddenly his whiskered face appeared in the crack at the edge of the door. "Ho ho ho!"

Katie and I squealed and bounced. She forgot all about going to the bathroom. All she cared about now was getting to the tree. Within minutes came the burp of the percolator. The odor of Dad's Doral wafted down the hall. It wouldn't be long now. As soon as he paid his morning visit to the john, we'd be good to go!

Christmas mornings in the Hubbell house were pure chaos. It was hard to rein us in from attacking the pile of colorfully wrapped gifts beneath our tree—it was one of the few times of year we got anything new. We would sprint to the living room, drop to our knees in our threadbare pajamas, and toss packages until we found our own gifts. After devouring everything under *our* tree, sometimes we'd be led into Grandma Nelson's part of the house; there would be gifts in there as well. One year, a red bicycle awaited me, and Katie, a dollhouse. This year the only thing I wanted to find—anywhere—was that Malibu Barbie.

We heard Anne and Janie's voices in the kitchen; Dad said he was about ready. That was all we needed. Before he even made it to the bedroom to lift the lock, Katie and I both gave the door a good yank. The wire hook gave way, and the door swung wide. We burst out and clambered past him, all his planning for naught. Katie was screaming. I was screaming. Mom was laughing about the broken lock.

I dove under our glistening tree, its bubble lights just beginning to simmer, seeking the first gift I could find addressed to me from Santa. It seemed I found everyone else's before I finally uncovered my own. I tore at it, hoping I'd chosen the right one. Thank god for Santa! It was the doll I'd been praying for: Malibu Barbie, dressed in a light-blue, one-piece bathing suit. "It's her! It's her!"

"What'd ya get?" Mom asked. She had roosted behind us on the couch in her housecoat and scuffs. She was sipping coffee from a steaming cup of white milk glass with gold trim and a leafy wheat pattern.

"Malibu Barbie!" I spun and held it high. "Santa brought it!" Katie pressed against me, ogling the contents of the pink bubble pack.

"She's gonna be cold," Dad said, and he and Mom laughed. They were always happy on Christmas; beer was never allowed.

My new Barbie was outta sight. She had tanned skin and long blonde hair. Atop her head perched a pair of round sunglasses tinted lilac. She was real mod. She didn't come with street clothes, only a miniature terry-cloth towel with fringed ends in bright yellow. Barbie clothes were expensive, and I'd left them off my list intention-ally—just in case I was asking too much. I didn't want to take any chances.

When most of the gifts were unwrapped, someone uncovered a remaining one addressed to me. It had been pushed behind the tree stand, its top sprinkled with fallen needles. I could smell the balsam scent as I slid it toward me—Santa breath. "It's from Gramma," I said.

"Oh," Mom said. "I was wondering what happened to that one."

Inside the wrapping paper was a plain white shoebox and, within, layers of handmade Barbie clothes. There was a red overcoat with miniature pearly buttons on the placket; a crocheted winter hat; a blue jumper; pajamas; pedal pushers; two pairs of culottes; a glittery blouse and pencil skirt; and, at the bottom of the pile, a bridal ensemble that included a white lace dress with a veil and a pink bridesmaid's gown with a shawl. I would never have asked for so much.

A day or so passed. I was in Mason for the remainder of Christmas break. I stood in the kitchen while Gramma prepared supper. "Did you like the brooch?" I asked.

"Oh, yah. That was real pretty. I'll have to get all dolled up one of these days." She gave me one of her click-winks. Gram was a real "looker" when she dressed up. Even Mom said so.

"I love my Barbie clothes, Gram. How'd you know I needed them?"

She shrugged. "Your ma thought that might be a good idea. She just had a feeling." She said she'd stashed some money aside and had a woman she knew make them for her. Like Mom and Dad, Gramma didn't have much money. The thought leapt up and nipped me, smack dab in the middle of my ribcage, in the place where I laid my palm for the Pledge of Allegiance. I didn't like the idea of Gram spending what little she had on doll clothes. For a moment—just one moment—I wished she hadn't spent her money on me that way.

INSEPARABLE

We headed for Gramma's as always on Friday after school. My worldly possessions were at my side: a brown paper sack with a change of clothes in one hand, my green Barbie doll case in the other. I was alone in the backseat of the Bel Air. My sisters were both in high school and rarely stayed at Gramma's anymore. They had grown more interested in their friends and in boys.

"Give Gram a kiss for me," Janie had said earlier as I prepared to leave.

"You should come," I said.

"I have to babysit."

They always seemed to have something going on these days. Ahead, I could see Gram's house, its white lap siding anchored by poor rock mortared together in a mishmash pattern. Such foundations were common in the area. In the mining days, if stone lacked ample ore, it was christened "poor rock" and tossed among the discards to be used for other purposes, like Gram's house.

Mom, my driver that day, would barely have been able to see over the steering wheel if not for the old bed pillow she sat on. She'd been born at home, a preemie, not even breathing at first. Her Aunt Florence had attended the delivery. Somehow Florence knew to breathe into Mom's tiny mouth until her blue body let out a wail. "After that I never stopped," Mom said once. She was warmed in a drawer in the kerosene lamplight and nourished with canned commodity milk. Despite these efforts to help her thrive, she was still too small, in my opinion, to be operating a motor vehicle. Nonetheless, a flick of her wrist made the blinker tick as we rolled down the steep drive to a smooth stop. The ground below crunched in the thick tread of snow tires, which would be out of season before long. *Got everything?* Mom would ask each time we arrived. *Did you grab your toothbrush like I asked?*

I leapt out of the sedan, darted across the sloppy drive, and bounded up the porch steps with Mom trailing behind. The iron latch on the four-plank door released from its carriage with a *schlik* and the door shuddered open. I stepped inside the dimly lit shed, a space of prewelcome that smelled of lumber and rock salt. Gram released the golden deadbolt on the front door. The brass throw snapped from the jamb, and there she stood. More familiar scents beckoned me inward: Creamette with tomatoes and bacon for supper; wood burning in the stove directly ahead; and the softer, more chemical odor of the oil burner in the front room. Over it all hung the veil of Pall Malls, the subtle tartness embedded in Gram's cotton housedress, her baggy sweater, her apron, and the skin of her sueded cheek, which I kissed as I entered. I inhaled it all. To me, it was home.

"I'm back!" I said, setting my things down on the mat. I smiled up at her. She wasn't much taller than me anymore.

There was a warmth in her Easter-egg eyes as she tousled my hair. "Did you wipe your feet?" She always asked that question in the winter.

I returned to the shed, stomped my boots, and swept the slush from their toecaps. Back inside, I stood beside the table, my elbow propped on its surface, my chin resting in my palm. Absently, I watched Gram and Mom making small talk—the old English woman with her broad hips, short waist, and low-slung bust; the young Chippewa who looked like a movie actress with her thick black hair pinned atop her head, a beauty mark on her cheekbone. People sometimes said Mom reminded them of Elizabeth Taylor. I had seen the actress once in a photo, dressed as Cleopatra. In a way, Mom's features were exotic like that. I saw their point.

There was often tension between them—Mom and Gram. I felt it. Though I had only garnered bits and pieces of their past while eavesdropping on conversations—a bad habit of mine, as Gramma had pointed out on numerous occasions—I knew Gram had been unkind to Mom in the past. I knew that when my father first brought home his young bride, Gramma resented her. She resented her daughter-in-law's presence in the house, perhaps resented being usurped as the most important woman in my father's life, even resented Mom's race. And when my father died, Gramma resented Mom for that as well.

All that lay dormant now, as an accord had been reached for the sake of the grandchildren. We carried her son's name—his DNA. Some of us had his fleshy nose, his sideways grin, a Cupid's bow on our upper lip. He lived on through us, a presence Gramma cherished. But her love came to embrace everything we were. *Be proud of who you are*, she would say of our Indian blood. *Be proud of where you come from.* There was no resentment in that.

When Mom remarried, she introduced yet another layer to their complex relationship: Derry. He was not always in favor of our stays in Mason, though I didn't know why. Sometimes he flat-out objected. At times Mom yielded, but on one recent occasion she had not.

"She can live without Mason for awhile," Dad said one Friday afternoon while I prepared to leave. I was in my bedroom digging through my drawers when I heard him. I froze, waiting for what came next. "She comes back every week too big for her britches. I don't know what goes on there, but I'm sick and tired of this bullshit."

Soldiers must cuss a lot; I figured that's where Dad learned it. Not only did he swear when he was angry, but when he was happy, when he was sad, when he had nothing more to say. It was just his way.

"*I told you.*" I heard Mom's voice, agitated and strained, the vowels drawn out as her temper rose. "That's Jack's mother! She needs those kids." She padded past my room to the back door at the end of the hall. Mom was spry and walked twice as fast as anyone else, though her legs were half the size.

"You and your Jack!" Dad shouted. I was sure his face was red by now, and his bald spot too. I couldn't say I blamed him. For Mom, no one would ever quite live up to the memory of my dead father—a fact that made my stepdad jealous. I think Dad really wanted a family—our family—but we'd all come with a lot of baggage. "Dammit the hell! Jack is gone. He was always gone, Margaret!" His statement wasn't far off the mark. Though I had been too young to remember for myself, I'd heard it said my real dad wasn't around much.

Mom stood just outside my room. "Don't you *ever* talk about him like that," she said. She was seething on the other side of the wall as I sat dead still, afraid for even the sound of my breath to be heard. "Just keep your damn mouth shut!" There was a thud against the wall, followed by the slam of the back door.

"And you can go to hell!" Dad bellowed down the empty hall.

And that was the end of that.

Things were not always that volatile, though. As I stood in Gramma's kitchen, I was grateful that our most recent departure from Hubbell had been a quiet one. Mom and Gram seemed relaxed as they chatted about mundane topics such as the weather, the price of groceries, and my dental hygiene.

"Okay then," Mom concluded. "I better get back to that brood in Hubbell." She offered a complex smile, tight and quivering. It was hard to gauge Mom's smiles—whether they were rooted in real happiness. "Give Mama a kiss bye-bye." She extended an arm in my direction.

I went to her. "Bye," I said, and kissed her cheek—warm, brown, fragrant.

"We'll see you Sunday. Be a good girl and take care of your gramma."

She had left the car running, but I heard the clunk of the transmission as it shifted into reverse. At last, Gramma and I—like Felix and Oscar, the Odd Couple—were free to pick up where we had left off the previous weekend.

Gramma busied herself in the kitchen while I made my way through the house for my first chore. Still in my boots and unzipped coat, I passed through the front room, paused beside the bird cage, and trilled in a way I'd heard Gram do countless times before. She had a low voice—almost a purr, like Lauren Bacall's—but she spoke to her canary in a high, singsong tone. *Pretty Bird, Pretty Bird*, she'd say, and it would respond in like fashion.

Pretty Bird's real name should have been Pretty Bird II. Pretty Bird I had passed on years ago. (My aunt said the bird's name was originally Billy Bird, but I had never heard Gram use it.) It was the same with the marmalade cat. Baby the First had been discovered dead on the roadside by a neighbor across the highway. When Gramma was ready for another cat, along came the similarly marmalade Baby II.

I never questioned why she gave her pets the same names as their predecessors, though I recognized it was unusual. I figured maybe Gram had experienced too much loss not to replace whatever she could.

"Pretty Bird never talks to me like he does you," I said to Gram.

"He knows which side his bread's buttered on," she said.

Beyond the front room was a small alcove that had originally served as the main entry. Its unused door led to an old porch fronting the highway. The door lacked weather stripping, and one could feel cold drafts creeping in around its frame like the bony fingers of a corpse. Directly across from the alcove stood my destination: the steep, narrow stairwell leading to the second floor. A floor-length curtain draped from a thin piece of rope strung across the stairway entrance, its floral, olive fabric drawn to keep the heat from funneling up the chimney-like enclosure. I pulled it aside. Each Friday afternoon, this was my job: I emptied the white, enameled chamber pots. One had been Grampa Otten's. It had a sturdy metal lid that looked like a supper plate and was wide and deep, its rim pencil-thin and cold as a skate blade. Sometimes on winter mornings, if you peed in Grampa's pot when it was empty, steam rose up. I mostly avoided using that one. I preferred the shallower pot with the plastic lid, which was kid-sized. They both sat side by side on the steps behind the curtain, so we didn't have to squat too low. It was the early seventies, but Gramma's 1917 mining home still lacked an indoor bathroom; in recent years we'd begun to rely on the chamber pots instead of the outhouse, which had since become a haven for flies and spiders. (Nothing was worse than a horsefly bite to a bare backside.)

I hoisted a pot. On the step around its base I noticed something—a halo of sorts; scant traces of dried liquid. It was spattered about on the tread like fading puzzle pieces, the stains almost translucent. I stared. It was unlike Gramma to be untidy. She must not have noticed, because she would have cleaned up after herself. I tore some tissue from the roll and wiped hard at the spots. I hated to admit it, but Gram was getting old.

Later that night, she and I lay in the creaky bed against the cold plaster walls. We read in the dim light of a single bulb, which hung from a porcelain socket overhead. My eyes stung, and I squinted at the page. I had packed along a Nancy Drew mystery from the school library. Gram read from her stack of *True Detective* magazines, which she kept below the TV tray at her bedside. Dad wouldn't like that I could see all their adult-themed cover art and raunchy headlines. He was particular about that kind of thing. He never let us miss a holiday special, but he wouldn't let me watch *Here's Lucy*. I could only watch the opening credits because I liked the dancing marionette. Other than that, he didn't care for the content. I learned it was best not to mention what I watched on television in Mason or which magazines were next to Gramma's bed.

Our bedroom was at the front of the house, on the highway side, and, as we lay there, I could hear cars coming from a good half mile down the stretch. I could feel the rumble of their tires on the pavement, the mushroom of vibration as they drew nearer. Headlights bled through the brittle window shades and traced a bright, hypnotic horizon from one corner of the room to the other.

Gram finished reading her article and fished through her reserve pile looking for something new. Baby leapt up on the mattress. We raised the covers so he could worm his way down to the foot of the bed where he slept each night, warming our feet like a misplaced mukluk. "Lucky thing we got that cat," Gram said. She must have been cold.

I lost interest in my book and handed it to her to set aside. "I'm sleepy," I said, and rolled over.

She gazed at the book's cover. "You like these Nancy Drews?"

"Mm hmm."

"Maybe next week when you come you can bring me one. I'm running outta stuff to read here."

I thought I should ask her to select a title from the handy list on the back cover, but sleep mired me, sweet and syrupy. I mumbled agreement. Lulled by the distant whir of rubber on M-26, I snuggled close against her. Maybe Dad was right. Maybe I *could* live without Mason—but I could never live without Gramma.

SUPERSTITIONS AND PREMONITIONS

I worried about black cats. Both Mom and Gramma were superstitious, and despite my attempts to dispel the myths, a few soaked in. I knew where Mom's superstitions came from—L'Anse was still very much a part of her—and I assumed Gram had inherited hers from the Cornish. People from the old country were like that—at least, that's what I had deduced from watching TV. If we ever mentioned seeing a black cat, Gram would need to know if it had crossed the road in front of us—that was a bad sign. If there were three knocks at the door, that was a bad sign. Often, as she sat on the couch beside me, her palm would itch. *Oh!* she'd say. *There's money coming.* But if the other palm itched, it meant company was coming.

Like Mom, Gramma also believed in visions. She believed in premonitions, ghosts, and reincarnation too. We had to be very choosy about which bugs we swatted inside her house. We didn't like flies, bees, or spiders, so we could smash those (except for the daddy longlegs, which was clearly harmless and sweet), but moths, june bugs, and certain other insects were shown the door instead. After all, you never knew which deceased relative they might be.

At Gram's I learned that loved ones could come back not only as insects but also as animals. This lesson occurred when Mom and I arrived in Mason one Friday afternoon for my usual visit. As Gram had asked the week before, I'd packed two Nancy Drew mysteries in my bag—one for each of us. The car rolled down the drive and came to a stop only feet from the porch steps. I was surprised to see a white retriever mix pacing about nearby. It looked excited to greet us.

"Ooh, be careful, Trese," Mom said. "Watch that stray."

I climbed out of the car and stood still a moment to test its nature. It sauntered over and rubbed against my legs. I reached down to pat its head. "It's nice, Ma!"

"It's probably dirty." Her nose wrinkled, and she whispered as if she didn't want the dog to hear. "Don't touch it." Mom viewed everything as a potential hazard.

We headed up the steps and through the shed, where Gramma was unlocking the kitchen door. She welcomed us in but seemed preoccupied. She was talking faster than usual, rushing the conversation. She fiddled with the grate on the wood stove, shifting her weight from one foot to the other. I figured *The Secret Storm* was really good that day and she wanted to get back to it.

"Where'd *that* come from?" Mom asked of the dog.

"Oh, it just showed up one day this week. I can't get rid of it."

"You never know about strays and rabies," Mom said. "I hope you're not feeding that thing. It'll never leave."

"Nah. I just gave it a few scraps and some water. Can't let it starve to death."

Mom headed back out to the car, shooing the dog away in short, high-pitched commands. "Go on. Go on now. Git!"

When Mom had driven off, Gramma scurried to the kitchen window and pulled back the flounced cafe curtain. "Trese," she whispered, motioning me toward her, her eyes fixed on the porch steps. "I think that's your dad."

"My dad?" I joined her at the window. It seemed my father paid a lot of visits to the Mason house, but Gramma always said we should fear the living—not the dead. When I looked out, all I saw was the white dog sitting near the bottom step, panting.

"He showed up a few days ago, and he hasn't left this yard since. Why would a white stray show up in my yard?" She appeared to consider her question. "Mark my words— that's Jackie. That's your dad."

It wasn't for me to argue. If she believed it was my dad, then maybe it was. She was the adult. We watched the dog for a moment or so, then went about our chores as usual.

The following week when Mom dropped me off, the white dog was nowhere to be seen. I looked all around. "What happened to the dog, Gram?" I asked after Mom left.

"Strangest thing," she said. "It hung around here all week. Nice dog. Wouldn't hurt a flea. Lil stopped by and she thought I should call the sheriff about it. I told her I'd call, but later that day he was gone. He musta sensed I was gonna call and high-tailed it outta here." She looked out the kitchen window. "I wasn't really gonna call." She seemed lost in thought, then nodded her head. "I'll just bet that was Jackie."

It had been a couple weeks since the white dog disappeared from Gramma's yard. She and I sat playing rummy on the bed in Grampa's old room. We sometimes did that if we didn't feel like reading—either that or checkers. She sat with her legs draped over the edge of the mattress, ankles crossed, the outer sides of her cordovan loafers resting on the floor. I lay on my belly toward the bottom of the bed so she couldn't see my hand. Gramma was a card shark—I needed all the advantage I could get.

She laid down three cards near her thigh and discarded one. I looked over my hand and checked the discards to see if there was anything I needed. Gramma waited, staring at the floor, flexing her feet. She'd been quiet all day. "I don't think Gramma's gonna be here much longer," she said.

My heart flopped and fluttered. I hated when it did that. "Don't say that, Gram." I tried to go on with the game, assessing my cards.

"I had a premonition. It was right there on the floor." She laid her cards face up on the bed. I could see her whole hand. I tried not to look, but the little red kings and black queens stared at me with vacant eyes.

"What'd you see? Where?" I drew my knees up under me and sat upright. The discard pile slid out of alignment. I figured it didn't much matter. The game was clearly over. She was still staring at the floor, so I looked down too, wondering if I could see it, fearful of what it might be.

"The other day I woke up in the morning and it was sunny out. I saw it right there." She pointed at the floral lino-leum rug, her face gaunt. "It was a wreath...with little white flowers...a death wreath...with a ribbon. There was a black snake curled up in it."

My skin prickled. I scooted closer, craving her warmth, her weight to ground me. I was used to her premonitions, but I didn't always like them. At times they were funny, at times mysterious, but sometimes they were just plain spooky, like now.

"The snake spoke to me. He told me. He said, 'Blanche, your time has come.' It was right there when I woke up in the morning." She drew a circle in the air with her index finger, tracing the outline of the image in her memory.

Tears welled up and I flushed. Was I scared? Was I mad at her for talking like this? I didn't know. I rested my hand on her shoulder to soothe her. "It was just a bad dream, Gram." I moved my face toward hers, blocking her line of vision to the scary spot on the floor. "You just had a bad dream." Could she hear my heart beating? I didn't want to add fuel to the fire.

Shortly after that, we both crawled into bed. Before long I heard the rhythm of her breath in sleep, wispy and delicate in her elongated nostrils. I lay awake beside her, waiting for my sleep to come as well, but it was taking its time. Whenever I closed my eyes I saw a halo of red; fading puzzle pieces taunted. I saw the stains I had found on the steps weeks ago.

IN LIKE A LION

The slop of spring was upon us. Despite the mess, we embraced the season, shedding our mittens and unbuttoning our coats. Hatless, I hopped off the rumbling Blue Bird bus after school and tromped through the back door of the Hubbell house, ready to head to Gramma's for the weekend. I hung my coat on the coat rail and kicked off my boots. They hit the drywall with a hollow thud, adding to the water stain on the white wall. All the snow outside was giving way to slush, so it was impossible to make it from the bus stop to our house with clean galoshes. Our teacher said that with any luck March might go out like a lamb.

"Hi, Mom!" I could see her down the long hallway. She was working in the kitchen.

She looked up briefly. "Trese, you're not going to your gramma's this weekend. She's sick."

"Aw." That was not at all the news I was expecting, but it had happened before. Usually if Gram had a bad cold or flu, she would ask that I stay home; she wouldn't feel up to fixing meals. Once, a couple years earlier, she had been painting one of her rooms. She was standing on a kitchen chair and stepped off into the paint tray, spraining her ankle. I didn't get to visit her for a couple weeks that time. My older sisters had to go do the chores.

"Your sister's gonna go this weekend," Mom said from the kitchen.

Anne didn't go to Mason much at all anymore. She had a boyfriend and a job. That was how she'd managed to get her cool bell-bottoms and the moccasins with the fringe at the ankle. I figured Janie would be the one to go. She had aspirations of becoming a nurse. She even volunteered as a candy striper at the hospital in Calumet. Janie was old enough to fix her own meals and could fix something for Gramma as well. She could probably even warm Gram's thimble of Mogen David, which she liked whenever she was sick. The only thing I could make on the stove at Gramma's was tea.

In my bedroom, I stacked my two new library books on the bureau. Book checkout was always on Friday, and I had selected two more mysteries—one for me and one for Gramma. I figured I could hold onto hers for next weekend. Gramma was a fast reader. The last one I brought her she'd finished in one weekend.

It had been a couple weeks since I'd seen Gram. She'd been really sick. The day was bright for a change, and once again I stood at the end of the hall after school, slung my sloppy boots from my feet, and peeled off my Thurner's bread bag boot liners. Easter was only weeks away, and soon we wouldn't have to wear snow boots at all. That was always something to look forward to—liberation. Earlier that week, I'd trudged through the marsh searching for pussy willows for Mom, but they'd yet to bloom. Nonetheless, Dad would soon pry open the cracked wooden door to the cellar and spring our bikes from cold storage. The slush would melt and trickle downhill, probably into Torch Lake, and we kids would take back the roads.

The Hubbell house was uncharacteristically quiet that afternoon. Mom was gone. I grabbed a couple no-name sandwich cookies from a tray and sat in the living room watching TV. *Batman* reruns were my favorite, but once in a while I still watched *Mr. Rogers' Neighborhood*. That show was like a hug—sometimes I needed it.

Before long I heard commotion at the end of the hall. Mom was back.

"Where'd you go?" I asked.

"Oh." She seemed flustered when she saw me. "Trese, I need to tell you some news." You'd think I was a grown-up or something. It was unlike anyone to *tell me news*. I didn't say anything, so she continued. "Your gramma had to go into the hospital."

Several days later, we had eaten supper and said goodbye to Dad. He was going to stay with Katie and Chris for the evening while we went to the hospital to visit Gramma. Mom, my two older sisters, and I climbed into the Bel Air and drove the ten miles to Hancock, where we parked beside St. Joe's Hospital, a tall, V-shaped tower along the Portage with a giant cross over its portico. All Mom's kids had been born in that hospital. Two had died there as well.

I'd begged Mom to take me along that evening, even though I had only just turned ten and wouldn't be permitted beyond the lobby. (You had to be twelve years old to visit patients.) Mom didn't see the sense of it but finally agreed. Perhaps she knew it would make me feel better to be in the same building as Gram. As we walked through the glass doors and ascended the slippery terrazzo steps, she reminded me of the rules. "Remember, Trese. You have to wait in the lobby."

"I know. But remember? You said you'd tell her I'm here."

"I'll tell her."

"And tell her I wanna see her, but I'm not allowed."

"She knows that, Trese."

"We'll tell her too," my sisters said. "If Ma forgets."

The three of them walked off down the dim corridor, their voices echoing. I sprawled across a stiff vinyl bench—maybe gold or yellow or almond—to wait, wallowing in envy of their maturity. The place smelled like Mom's laundry room. The walls were made of slabs of earth-colored stone with a swirling pattern; the floors were speckled like the ones at school. There was a nurse in a white uniform and pointy cap seated at a massive, wood-framed reception station at the top of the steps. It looked like the entrance to a big hotel, like something you'd see in a Jerry Lewis movie. The nurse paid no mind to me at all, so I was alone with my thoughts in the cavernous space. Beyond the tall plate-glass windows, darkness had fallen and donuts of mist encompassed the streetlights.

Upstairs, somewhere, lay Gramma. Since she'd entered the hospital, the news had gotten worse. Earlier that day, Mom had told me Gramma had cancer. I knew cancer was bad, because my brother had died of it. But he was a little boy. Gramma was full-grown. Stronger. I thought she could fight it.

"Is she going to die?" I asked, just in case Mom knew.

"I don't know. She's very sick. You should pray for her."

I did just that at night in the top bunk. We were supposed to kneel when we prayed, but our bedroom floor was too hard and cold for that. I trusted God would understand. He took care of kids.

I had talked to Gramma on the telephone after school earlier in the week. I stood by the wall phone as Mom dialed the number and asked for her room. "There's someone who wants to talk to you," she said, and handed me the big, chunky receiver.

"Gramma?" No one immediately answered, but I could hear noises on the other end. I was holding the receiver with two hands, one of them partially covering the mouthpiece. I looked to Mom, and she moved my hand out of the way.

Usually I knew how to talk on the phone. I must have been nervous.

"Say hi," Mom said.

"Hi, Gramma," I said again, a little louder.

"Hi, honey." She sounded tired, her voice ragged, like she was getting over a bad cold.

"How are you?" I asked. She seemed so far away. A mass blocked my windpipe, like I'd swallowed a snowball.

"Gramma's hanging in there."

We didn't say much more that day. She was too tired.

I lay in the solitude of the hospital lobby. Would the nurse across the way even notice if I disappeared? Would she wonder where I'd gone if I snuck up the stairwell and searched for Mom and my sisters? Wherever I found them, I'd find Gramma, I was sure. I got butterflies; it wasn't my nature to defy authority. I stared up at the ceiling, trying to talk myself into it. Maybe I could be like Joe Mannix from the TV show. Gram liked that show. She liked mysteries. I pictured myself running down empty hospital halls, darting around corners, dashing into stairwells. Avoiding discovery. I could do it. I just needed to work up to it. Shortly afterward, however, I heard the echo of familiar voices in the long corridor. Too late. Mom and my sisters were rounding the corner.

"Ready?" Mom asked. She stuck her arm out and wiggled her pretty manicured fingers. I didn't expect I'd ever have nails like that. Mine would always look like Gram's.

I slid off the bench and fell in line with the rest of them. Mom stared at the ground as she walked toward the exit. Obviously, I would not be seeing Gramma this time.

Monday, April 9: a few days since I'd sat in the lobby of St. Joe's, fruitlessly fantasizing about breaking hospital rules. I came home to find the house once again eerily quiet. Things at home had gone topsy-turvy ever since Gramma entered the hospital. I'd sure be glad when she went home and things got back to normal. Dad showed up eventually and fixed supper for Katie, Chris, and me. My two older sisters were nowhere around.

It was dark outside when I heard Mom coming in the back door. I peeked around the corner. She was cradling Baby, the marmalade cat. I was confused. Dad didn't like cats. He was a dog person.

"You brought Baby?" I asked.

Mom set the cat down on the linoleum. "Trese…" she said. She was still wearing her coat. I saw her face clearly then; the fluorescent light of the kitchen illuminated her. Her eyes were big, lush raindrops, her nose swollen. She drew a shallow breath and looked over my shoulder at Dad for a fraction of a second. My spine stiffened. "Your gramma died today, honey."

Was she lying? I didn't believe her—wouldn't believe her. But her eyes were red with truth. I searched them for signs, combed her black irises, as beneath me the speckled floor lurched. The walls shrieked past at warp speed and the room blurred. It sucked out my breath and I pitched forward, clutching my stomach. Mom had shoved me into a hole, deep and dark. Legless, I plummeted. My head sought the cold slab, where it lay wreathed in numb limbs. All was black, but somewhere a raw, pitchy howling rose and echoed in the tiny cavern I'd created with my body. Then something warm and soft brushed against me. There was a gentle nudge against my head. It was Baby, come to comfort me. I drew him to me and sobbed into his tangerine fur. A little piece of Gramma—still living.

Mom crouched beside me. She rubbed my back and tried to console me, but I wept on. At some point she stood up and spoke to Dad, who was standing nearby. Through my tears I could see his boots with the washboard soles and the frayed hem of his work pants. They talked about me as if I wasn't there, as if I couldn't hear them, but I could.

"What should we do?" Mom asked. "I don't know what to do."

"Geez," Dad said, worry in his voice. "I don't know."

"Maybe we should call Lisa. Maybe she can talk to her."

So that's what they did.

March might have gone out like a lamb, but for me, April came in like a lion.

PART TWO

CHIPPEWAS AT BREAKFAST

In our family, dreams were lessons. You studied them. You learned from them. Sometimes you feared them. In the Hubbell house, dreams were often discussed at meals—symbols dissected, meanings digested. One morning I sat at the kitchen table eating soggy puffed wheat while my mother and sisters examined a dream.

"Then, when I opened the door, there was nothing there," Janie said.

I listened to their conversation despite my better judgement. Sometimes what I heard kept me up at night. Sometimes these secondhand dreams kept me from visiting the bathroom when I woke to a dark room. I'd fear sliding from my bunk, putting my feet on the floor. Scary dreams lurked under the bed. They hid in closets and beyond attic doors.

"Oh, no," Mom said. She could get riled up about dreams, whoever the dreamer. At times she had powerful dreams herself and sometimes visions too. Though she couldn't explain it, she knew it was the Chippewa in her.

That's how Chippewas were. We had little knowledge of those ways, but at a young age I'd assimilated the awareness that Indians not only dreamed the dreams of ordinary men, they dreamed the dreams of spirits too. Those were the dreams that made one take notice—the ones that held a message. This had become part of my belief system, but I thought I might not be Indian enough to have such dreams myself. To my recollection, I'd never had one.

Growing up off the reservation, it was a struggle to understand many of Mom's beliefs, which mirrored those of her mother and brothers. Every so often, we would all pile into the car and make the thirty-mile drive south to visit Grandma Woods in her apartment in L'Anse or Uncle Blue and his family, who lived in tribal housing in Baraga, where on the walls they'd labeled the globes of their late-sixties light fixtures with terms like "sun" and "moon"—like the stones of an ancient Medicine Wheel. Dad would never let us write on the walls like that, but Uncle Blue had his own set of rules.

Grandpa Woods had walked on years ago, and Grandma Woods had returned to live in L'Anse once Mom remarried. She had stopped drinking, too, and wasn't angry with Mom anymore. This made Mom happy and made it easier for us to visit her as well, but we didn't go often. Thirty miles was a long drive. Her apartment was small and modestly furnished and overlooked Keweenaw Bay. It was sunny and bright inside, with a linoleum-tiled floor—a tad institutional. On the wall, Grandma Woods had framed our school photos in a Corn King bacon box. She must have been very proud of us. She'd even kept the cellophane on the box, maybe to preserve the photos. I'd never seen anyone make a frame out of a bacon box before, though Gramma Bertineau had a cardboard frame that was printed to look like the real deal. Grandma Woods might have been poor, but she was resourceful.

Sober, our Indian grandma was sweet and giggly and a bundle of nervous energy, much like Mom. Whenever we came to visit, she would dart about her tiny kitchen and living area, extending offerings to make us more comfortable. Despite their past, Mom treated her with the utmost respect and was always fussing over her and worried about her health. We were naturally respectful as well, but there was a difference in the way I treated Grandma Woods from the way I was with Gramma Bertineau. I would never hang on Grandma Woods like I did my other gramma. Grandma Woods evoked a different type of respect—something more formal, perhaps because she always called me "granddaughter." Mom said Grandpa Woods had called me "granddaughter" too, though I was too young when he died to remember it.

Sometimes we'd bring Grandma Woods home with us to Hubbell, and she would stay a week or so. She was a soft, pudgy bowl of pudding not much taller than me who spoke with a thick tongue and languid lips, so I had to listen closely to her words. Like Uncle Blue, she had a dry sense of humor and a contagious, throaty chuckle. *Eii*, she would say. Her wide, round face smelled of Pond's Cold Cream and chewing tobacco, which she called snuff, and she always carried a Hills Bros. Coffee can as a spittoon. Her taupe skin was freckled with age spots, and her eyes were charcoal like her hair. She wore dresses with the hems at midcalf and oversized sweaters, her calves squeezed by beige, opaque stockings rolled at the knee, her feet usually in scuffs.

When Grandma Woods stayed over, she was always given the lower bunk where Katie usually slept. At bedtime, she would kneel on the cold faux-wood floor—where I *wouldn't* kneel—and pray the rosary. I would scoot to the edge of the bunk and peek over at the top of her bowed head. Though she prayed with the same cadences I'd learned in catechism, her beads clicking as she progressed, her sounds were a mix of English and her mother tongue—that of the Chippewa.

In her youth, Grandma Woods had been sent away to attend boarding school in Mount Pleasant in lower Michigan—an "industrial school," they called it—where she had felt totally alone. At Mount Pleasant, as with all Indian boarding schools, Grandma Woods was forbidden to speak her birth language. They wanted her to forget her Indian ways—to learn new ways—so they taught her English, but her tongue had never surrendered. I heard its rebellion in her recital of the rosary.

At Mount Pleasant she'd had a terrible accident—perhaps a blessing in disguise. She fell from the bleachers and spent weeks in the infirmary. The school superintendent wrote her father and said she had tripped over a chair. He assured him it was nothing serious—but it was. When the school could do nothing more to aid her recovery, she was sent home to heal, her lessons unfinished. Maybe that's why she seemed more Indian than Mom. More Indian than anyone else I'd met. Maybe that's how she'd managed to preserve her language. Mom said both Grandpa and Grandma Woods had spoken their language in the home, the only place it was safe to do so, but Mom was always afraid to speak it herself. Her parents had warned her never to use it beyond their door. She grew up relying on English, left home young, and forgot her first language, which she called "Indian." As a child I thought all Indians, regardless of tribe, spoke the same tongue.

Now, as I sat listening to Janie's dream, I could see my Grandma Woods's mannerisms in my mother. Oddly enough, Mom was a lot like my Cornish gramma too. In Mom's eyes, everything was a sign of something—an omen—just like it had been in Gram's house. They even shared the same first name, Margaret, though Gramma had gone by her middle name.

"What do you think *that* dream was about?" Mom asked, her eyes purled with emotion.

"I don't know," Janie said. "Maybe that I'm not making good choices?"

"Gives me the shivers." Mom shuddered and laughed. "Look at me." She held her arms out over the table. "I've got goose bumps!"

There were a lot of mornings like that in Hubbell. Most of the time the dreams were dark or cryptic—rarely were they pleasant. In our family good dreams were accepted gratefully, and the dreamers went on about their day. Bad dreams were something upon which one dwelled. There was a lot of dwelling.

Since Gram died, I had felt that life was all one big bad dream. I struggled in the weeks after the funeral, and though I was normally a good student, my grades suffered. Mom thought a vacation to Aunty Patsy's was in order. Patsy was Gramma's youngest daughter. Mom looked upon her more as a sister than a sister-in-law. She felt that way about both Gramma's remaining daughters. Patsy lived in West Virginia with her husband and two young sons. Jean, the oldest, had remarried years ago and now lived in Illinois with her family. I heard Mom and Dad talking about the trip south after I went to bed. "I think Trese could use the break," Mom said. "It might do her good to get out of here for awhile."

"Well, how're you gonna get down there?" Dad asked. He didn't sound too enthused about the idea.

"By bus. We'll take the Greyhound."

"How much is that gonna cost us?"

"We'll figure it out." It was clear Mom was annoyed with Dad's pessimism. Mom was annoyed with Dad a lot these days. "Maybe I'll take Chris with me too."

So on a cool May evening after dark, Dad, Mom, Chris, and I stood beside a silver Greyhound, which was parallel-parked outside the party store in Hancock. The odor of diesel congealed on the mist as Dad handed the driver our luggage. He slid it all into the belly of the bus. I held fast to my green Barbie case—that would remain with me. Shortly afterward we climbed aboard, and the brakes hissed and the engine belched as we jerked into motion. Dad stood below a streetlight looking forlorn as the coach roared away. We waved goodbye through the tinted windows, the bus's passing reflected in each storefront. I missed Dad already. He had his faults, but I loved him.

THE THIRD WHEEL

Had I known what was about to occur, I would've just as soon grieved at home.

I settled into the deep, firm seat of the Greyhound that May evening. Chris and I were seated together, me beside the window, him in the aisle seat closest to Mom. He flicked the chrome lid of the armrest ashtray a few times. *Snap. Snap. Snap.*

Mom reached over and brushed his hand away. *"Ca-ca,"* she said, crinkling her nose. Both she and Grandma Woods often used that term. For babies it meant feces. For kids it meant anything unsanitary. I always thought it was from the Indian language but learned sometime later it was not.

The bus crossed the Portage lift bridge, the inky water below reflecting the lights of its towers in squirmy, patriotic spikes. We lurched through the evening lull of Houghton and had just begun to pick up speed when we made an unexpected stop.

It happened along the highway just beyond Michigan Tech, the college on the east edge of town. I peeked out the window and saw a man waiting on the roadside, a chameleon: first red, then white, like the flashers on the bus. He was tall and thin with a mound of dark, fuzzy hair. He stood in the mist with a bag at his feet. He looked familiar to me. The driver swung the door open and he climbed aboard. The bus tilted a little to the right. I heard the thump of his feet on the grooved steps, felt the vibration in the floor. He maneuvered toward the back, stiff-arming his bag in front of him. I was surprised when he sat down with Mom across the aisle from Chris and me. But then she introduced him.

"Trese, this is my friend Luke," Mom said. Luke nodded and smiled. Wariness gripped me and I didn't respond. Mom filled the silence. "You remember Luke. He went smelting with us." Smelting was a popular spring ritual in which you netted tiny, shimmering fish—smelt—as they entered warming springs from the larger lakes. That's where I'd seen him before. I did remember smelting with him and some others one evening while Dad was out of town. Mom introduced him to Chris too. She said Luke was on his way to West Virginia just like us. "Isn't that nice?" she asked. I didn't think she expected an answer. She settled in beside the new passenger, chatting with him. Forgotten, I sulked in the darkness beside the cool window. Something told me this trip wasn't about *me* at all.

When the four of us arrived in West Virginia, it turned out Luke didn't have a place to go. He had to stay with us. Aunty

Patsy's place was too small for all of us, so we immediately rented a compact, blue-and-white-striped trailer house a few miles away. It was fully furnished.

"How long are we gonna stay here?" I asked Mom as we unpacked our few things.

"Oh, I don't know. Awhile," she said. "Maybe you could finish school here."

Finish school here? I didn't know we were planning to stay *that* long. I thought it was just a vacation. I hadn't even said goodbye to my friends in Hubbell. Wouldn't they wonder where I'd gone? What about Dad? And my sisters? And what about Luke? Would he stay too? Something told me Dad wouldn't care for that one iota.

After that, out of loyalty to Dad, I set out to pretend Luke didn't exist. I was a snot to him—the first adult I'd ever ignored. Surprisingly, Mom didn't correct me, although on occasion she did give me "the look."

Springtime in Parkersburg was like summer in the UP. The grass had greened and the trees had leafed out long before we arrived. It made for good outdoor fun. One sunny afternoon I was playing with the girl next door. She was a nice girl who never asked personal questions, so I never had to explain Luke to her. I never had to explain anything. She was safe to play with. I recall she had a large family and lived in a big white house—or maybe I thought she had a large family *because* she lived in a big house. It was an older home with an upstairs and a wide front porch. She had dark hair and dark eyes, just like me, but she wasn't an Indian. She never said as much, but I could tell. I never told her I was Indian. She never asked. There were a lot more brunettes in West Virginia, so I blended in.

"Let's trade Barbie clothes!" she suggested. We'd been playing Barbies that afternoon on her porch. She had a lot of nice, store-bought Barbie clothes. I was tempted by all the ruffles and fancy plastic shoes.

"Okay," I said. "I'll trade some stuff."

We negotiated our trades and exchanged clothing. Afterward, I packed up my Barbie case and headed back to the trailer. Once inside, I plunked down on the brown indoor-outdoor carpet of the living room floor, excited to go through my new things.

It didn't take long for regret to set in. Guilt was close on its tail.

I wanted Gram's handmade Barbie clothes back. I wanted my gold, glittery top and the navy blue pencil skirt. I wanted the culottes with the blue butterfly fabric. I gathered the things that had belonged to the neighbor girl, marched back across the yard, and knocked on her big black-tea door.

She answered my knock. "Hey," she said, smiling. "Did you forget something?"

Suddenly, this seemed like a bad idea. My gaze fell to the porch. "I don't like trading," I said to the wooden planks. "I shouldn't have done it. I want my old Barbie clothes back." I looked up at her then, the hard part over.

Her face fell. "You said you wanted to trade," she said. "A trade's a trade."

"I know, but my gramma gave me those clothes. I wasn't supposed to trade them."

She glared at me through the partially open doorway, then disappeared inside the house, leaving the door ajar. I remained where I was, feet numb, wondering where she was. She reappeared quickly, holding out the orphaned items. I snatched them from her, filling her empty hands with her things. "Thank you," I said, relieved to have my stuff back.

"You're an Indian giver," she said with a scowl, and shut the door in my face.

Had I been stung on the heart by a hornet, it couldn't have hurt worse. Maybe I should have kicked her. Or something. No one ever called me that besides my brother or sisters. How'd she even know I was an Indian?

After supper one evening, Mom, Chris, and Luke went for a walk. I stayed behind, visiting with an elderly neighbor. He had old hands and hair like Frosted Mini-Wheats. He reminded me of Grampa Otten, but with clearer speech. He lived opposite the neighbor girl who was still mad at me. I hadn't much cared for her calling me names, so I'd left her alone since that day.

The neighbor man's home was only one level, the roofline barely taller than me, the siding a cheerful sea-foam green.

He was a nice man who liked to do woodworking on a bare patch of lawn beside his house. He'd even made me a two-foot-tall wooden cutout of Uncle Sam and painted it up all fancy in red, white, and blue.

As I stood in a puddle of sawdust chatting with him that evening, I caught sight of Mom, Chris, and Luke walking up the road. Chris was up on Luke's shoulders. My heart hiccuped and my face flamed. I lost focus on my conversation. I wanted to holler at Chris to get down. I wanted to holler at Luke too. *You're not our dad!* I wanted to say. *You don't get to do that! Only our dad does that!*

But Chris looked like he was enjoying the piggyback ride. My heart folded up and my frame sank, like a rag doll left out in the rain. I hoped he wouldn't forget his *real* dad.

I awoke in the night in the trailer. The gray light from the kitchen bled through the open doorway and spread like death across the bedroom floor. Chris and I shared the room, the only bedroom. He was asleep beside me. I don't know where Mom slept, or Luke for that matter, but neither was asleep now. I could hear them in the kitchen, could hear Mom's growls and howls—a coyote caught in a snare. I could hear Luke trying to tamp it down, trying to lasso the rage, like Dad sometimes did. There was a crash just beyond the door, the clang of metal hangers and the thump of rubber soles against thin walls. One of them had fallen into the coat closet. Two more feet and they'd be in our room. Terrified,

I wished for Anne and Janie. I pulled the blanket over my head and lay like a plank, melting into the mattress, the only place I could hide.

That's all I recall about that night. The episode must have passed quickly and without further incident, because I fell back to sleep. Sleep was always a good escape—if you could manage it. When I awoke the next morning, Luke was gone. It was a lot like Gramma's house when Flint disappeared. Mom didn't offer any explanation—and I didn't ask. I always pretended Luke didn't exist anyway, so his absence was fine by me.

That same week a dozen red roses appeared on the table. Dad had sent them.

"I have a big surprise!" Mom said that day. "The whole family is moving down here!"

"To West Virginia?" I asked.

"Yeah! We're all gonna live here together! I have to go and help 'em pack up the house."

"Daddy too?"

"Yeah, your Dad too," she said with a smirk.

"Yay!" I exclaimed, jumping up and down, arms in the air. I couldn't believe that Dad—a staunch Michigander— was moving to West Virginia! I couldn't have been more relieved if I'd just walked through the automatic doors of an air-conditioned Kroger's on a hot day. "Daddy's coming!" I cheered. I looked at Chris. "Daddy's coming, Chris!" He started jumping too, mimicking me, bouncing around the tiny kitchen and living area.

I couldn't wait to see my family again and to have Dad back. At the time, I assumed Luke was gone for good—but that story wasn't over yet either.

HOPE ALONG THE OHIO

What began as a brief respite from grief mutated into a two-year immersion in misery.

In late May, Mom and Chris returned to Michigan to prepare for the move to West Virginia. I remained in the care of Aunty Patsy, trying to finish up the fourth grade. Mom had enrolled me in school despite my protests. She didn't want me to miss out like she had when she was young.

"Why do I have to go to school here?" I asked. "The year's almost over."

"You have to go to school, Trese," she said. "You don't wanna flunk, do you?"

I didn't even like the sound of the word *flunk*. Reluctantly, I agreed to go. I moved in with my aunt and uncle, who lived with their two young sons, Kenneth and Matt, in a small, pistachio-colored trailer. There was a parking pad out front where Uncle's red Datsun pickup roasted (the sun in Parkersburg felt much warmer than sun in the UP). When I first entered their home, something familiar caught my eye.

On a table beside the couch sat Gramma's record player. My breath snared on a rib and my eyes stung as I stared at it. After a bit, I ran my fingers across its smooth plastic. Though it had only been weeks since Gram died, already it felt like a lifetime. Everything I knew had been turned on its head. At last, here was something recognizable. "This was Gramma's, eh?" I said to my aunt.

"Yep. That used to be Mom's all right." She was putting groceries away in the kitchen, singing a country-and-western song. She dreamed of singing professionally and was always practicing her skills. She had a good voice.

There were only two bedrooms in my aunt's trailer, so at night I slept on the couch in the living room, my head right below Gramma's record player. Usually my uncle woke first and was off to work before the rest of us were out of bed. One morning, however, there was a shift in the routine. The house was quiet when I awoke, the living room warm and golden as a raisin. The trailer's aluminum skin was soaking up June's morning sun. I hadn't heard my uncle leave for work, so I tiptoed through the kitchen and peeked into their bedroom. It was cozy in there. Light seeped through the lined curtains with a warm, chocolatey hue. I could make out two shapes nestled on the mattress, their hips spooned one against the other.

"Uncle," I whispered.

Two heads popped up. "Uh?" He turned to me over his shoulder.

"Don't you have to go to work today?"

He cranked his neck to see the alarm clock at their bedside. "Uh oh," he said. He flipped the covers aside and flung his white legs over the edge of the bed. "Good thing you woke me up."

"Thanks, hon," Aunty Patsy said, her voice muffled. She was closest to the wall.

I retreated to the living room, where I curled up on the couch again to keep out of his way. I figured this was what it was like to be Anne or Janie. Responsible.

My aunt and uncle were good to me during my stay, but I was homesick. This condition was accompanied by headaches, which began shortly after Mom left for Michigan. My strange new school seemed to exacerbate the ailment. I would go to class, but by late morning I would find myself in the nurse's office, staring down at my feet on the green-tiled floor, battling a mix of loneliness and guilt. The nurse would call my aunt and she would come check me out for the day. Once, after she picked me up, I sat with her at the Burger Chef downtown. We ordered hamburgers with french fries for lunch, a real treat.

"I don't know why I keep getting headaches," I said. I was more or less wondering out loud while we munched on our fries and watched the bustle of downtowners beyond the window.

"Maybe you're just lonesome," Aunty Patsy said. "Missin' your mom. Y'all'll be back together again soon." My aunt had developed a new dialect since she'd left the Copper Country. Now she used words like *y'all* and *fixin'*. No one spoke like that in Mason, where she had grown up, but she had married young, left Gramma (and her beer) behind, and moved on long ago. Drinking drove people away like that.

"I wish they'd hurry up and come back."

"Won't be much longer. Hang in there, hon."

School was finally out for the summer. I don't know how, but I managed to be promoted to the fifth grade. I awoke and pulled on my red knit hot pants and black lace-up shoes with the tall, chunky heels. My aunt had bought the shoes for me at Payless. They were the first grown-up shoes I'd ever owned, and I wore them every day. I even learned to run and jump rope in them without twisting my ankles.

Ever since the second grade I'd felt deficient when it came to shoes. That Fourth of July, I'd participated in games down at the park beside the Hubbell firehall. In one race, all the kids would pile their shoes at one end of the park, then line up at the opposite end. They called it the Shoe Scramble. Some blue-shirted fireman (often a distant relative of ours) would blow a whistle and we'd rush to the pile, dig for our shoes, put them back on, and race to the finish. The first three kids across the line would win money—dollar bills. I won the first race and hoped to win the second, but as I was about to stuff my feet into my shoes, one of the teenage helpers yanked them from my hand, glowering at me. "You have to undo these," she said as she pried at the fasteners.

On that particular Fourth of July, I was wearing Frankenstein shoes—an old pair of black, boxy school shoes with buckles on the side. I'd worn them every day since the previous fall—they were the only shoes I owned—and I had never unbuckled them. I wasn't trying to cheat. I looked up at her in dismay, but suddenly there was Anne, snatching them back. "You can't unbuckle those shoes!" she said, her hippie hair blowing like a cape in the breeze. She looked like a superhero. "They'll fall apart."

She tossed them back to me where I sat frog-legged in the dandelions. I slipped them on my feet and dashed for the finish. I didn't win any money that race, but I did walk away with fresh insight: I was shoe poor.

I pranced around the trailer in my fancy platforms until my aunt emerged from her bedroom. "Is today the day?" I asked.

"Yep," she said, grinning. She was very pretty, and I liked looking at her. She had the same nose and smile as Gramma, the same coloring too. "Should be sometime this afternoon."

Deep down, the familiar roller coaster rumbled. My family was coming to get me!

The day seemed to drag, but as the fireflies warmed up their blinkers, Mom and Dad finally arrived. I'd been pacing back and forth from the highway to the trailer when at last I spotted their car. I skirted the ditch as fast as my legs would carry me. Beside me, the dusty Bel Air slowed, swiveled, and rolled down the gravel road toward my aunt's place. I waved my arms wildly and called out to them, my heart hammering.

My Dad's grin came into focus, along with my siblings' faces, plastered against the rear passenger window. They all waved back like a busload of kindergarteners. What a marvelous sight! The only sibling absent was Anne. She had chosen not to make the move. She was entering her senior year in high school and had moved in with a girlfriend's family instead. Like Aunty Patsy with Gramma, I think Anne needed a break.

When the car stopped and everyone tumbled out, the first person I reached was Dad. I threw myself at him and kissed his whiskered chin. He must not have shaved that morning. His left arm was sunburned and even more freckled from hanging out the window, and he smelled comforting, like Stuckey's coffee and cigarettes. "I missed you, Daddy!"

He gave me a squeeze. "Ho ho!" he laughed. "I missed you too!" Grinning, he laid his speckled hand atop my head, cigarette and all. "Christ, you're growing like a weed!"

Maybe it was my new shoes.

Our new life in West Virginia began in a rented mobile home. It sat next to a wide, open field of untended weeds in a park dotted with similar dwellings. Life there was a big contrast to what we'd known up north. The mobile home had pretty blue trim—fancy compared to the rambler in Hubbell, which had been economically sided with plain brown Celotex. Dad and Mom had left all our furniture in the Hubbell house, so we were stuck with the furniture that came with the mobile home. That was fancy too, but Dad didn't care for it. *Don't lean back in those chairs!* he'd bellow. *The damn things are barely glued together!* He wasn't accustomed to furnishings constructed of particle board. If he caught us jumping on the beds, he'd yell at us then too. *I'm not paying these people to replace these beds, so quit your damn jumping!*

Since Dad was so worried about the furnishings, we spent a lot of time outdoors. One sticky summer evening, I herded lightning bugs into a Miracle Whip jar while somewhere in the park Three Dog Night's "Shambala" played, accompanying the cicadas. We'd had a lot of mosquitos in the UP, but no cicadas. Their high-pitched chirr was new to us. It was reminiscent of the static on Grampa Otten's portable radio, so it was oddly soothing. Janie sat nearby, eyes closed, head swaying side to side, lost in the music. The neighbor kids were out with us too, and for the first time in a long time, I was having fun.

"I like it here," I said to Janie. "Do you?"

"Yeah, it's nice." I thought that was all she would say—Janie was the positive one. Tonight, however, there was more. "But I miss Anne…and my friends." She sighed, heavy and deep; her posture crumpled. I'd ripped off a bandage. Her loneliness oozed.

I looked away, not knowing what to say. Janie clearly needed Anne. I never consoled my older sisters. I didn't know how. They did that for *me*. After an uncomfortable silence, I changed the subject. "I didn't like being by myself," I said. "It was lonesome."

Fortunately, Janie seemed agreeable to redirection. "Me and Anne were worried about you," she said. She was sitting cross-legged—"Indian-style," people called it—picking at blades of grass near her toes. "It's better if we stick together."

Briefly I thought life might be good in West Virginia, but on the banks of the murky Ohio River, work was hard to come by. Mom had hoped they might earn a better living here than in Hubbell, but it turned out the Parkersburg economy wasn't much of an improvement. Dad and Mom both eventually found jobs, but the pay was low. Their drinking resumed soon after we settled in, too, and they didn't always go to work like they were supposed to. They started out with good intentions—"on the wagon," Mom called it—but the wagon soon lost a wheel.

Also, from what I'd gathered since the move, Luke was still somewhere in the picture. Sometimes, when Mom left the house, she didn't come home. Dad knew about Luke now too, and just as I'd suspected, he didn't like him any more than I did. Mom and Dad fought a lot about it.

One afternoon an argument broke out about him. Mom grabbed the car keys and ran out the door. I didn't like it when she left. I feared she'd never come back. Dad didn't do too well without Mom—Janie usually had to take over. I ran to the picture window and yelled at her to stop. My voice bounced off the glass and pummeled my face. I could barely see her over the big steering wheel. Our eyes locked before she backed out of the drive and sped away, Conway

Twitty and Loretta Lynn blaring from the car's speakers. Fear turned to tears. My cheeks grew steamy with heat and moisture, then anger. I didn't want to cry *for* her. I wanted to yell *at* her. I pounded my fist on the not-quite-finished desk Dad had built for her when she was planning to go to typing school.

"Don't waste your tears on her, Theresa," Dad said. He was standing near the kitchen, his undershirt tatty at the neck, his face red as Mom's taillights. "Your ma's not worth it." If that was true, I wondered, why did he stay married to her?

Money was another thing Mom and Dad fought about. We didn't have any. We had to keep switching houses. We moved four times within two years, each time to a different school, though most were within the same district. Our second summer in Parkersburg, we were living in a small, ranch-style house. It was a cute place, the last house on a dead-end street. There was a potato patch across the road, and sometimes Katie, Chris, and I would hang on the fence while the farmer tended his crop. Every so often, the farmer would walk over to us and hand us each a fistful of young potatoes, which we proudly brought home to Mom. She thought it was funny, but sometimes she was grateful to have something more to feed us.

One afternoon I was hanging around the kitchen table. I was hungry. I watched as Mom rifled through our bare cupboards, slamming doors and drawers. Dad waited nearby, holding his bucket hat in his hand, scratching his bald spot with the tips of his fingers. He knew when to stand clear. Mom had a temper.

"What are we gonna fix these kids to eat?" she asked. She was dragging her vowels out—a sure sign of agitation.

"We don't have much, do we?" Dad said.

"*Much*?" She flashed a seething glance. "There's nothing! Not a thing. We're all gonna starve to death here if this keeps up!" She was at the cupboard where we normally kept the dry goods. She pulled out a slim, yellow box, read the back label, and slapped the box down on the counter. "I guess I can make this."

"What's that?" he asked.

"Cornmeal mush."

I owned a goldfish while we lived in the ranch on Twelfth Avenue. Janie had bought it for me as a gift. The fat round fishbowl sat in the middle of the kitchen table we'd picked up secondhand. We all watched it as we ate our meals, making fish lips at it and gently tapping on the glass. I had named it Goldie, and it was my responsibility to clean its bowl and keep it fed. I'd been doing a pretty good job.

One afternoon, several months after Goldie's arrival, a ruckus broke out in the house. The drinking had fired up earlier in the day than usual. It must have been payday, because there was food in the cupboards and beer in the fridge. Empty cupboards had begun to seem almost desirable—if there wasn't money for food, there wasn't money for beer.

I sometimes grumbled in private to Janie when our parents returned from grocery shopping. Though I looked forward to a fresh box of Freakies cereal, I knew it came with a price. Janie tended to keep her feelings about such matters to herself. She preferred to look at life from a different angle and, like the Chippewa, believed in respecting her elders. Clearly, Janie was Chippewa through and through. I wondered how I'd ended up a mix.

When the fight broke out, my siblings and I all scurried to a bedroom and shut the door. If things got too rough, we could always scoot out the window and hang out with the bugs in the trees behind the house; we'd done that before. Beyond the door, things escalated, and before long came the cartwheeling of kitchen chairs and the piercing crash of glassware, like a carnival gone berserk.

Shortly after, Dad and Mom disappeared. We had no idea where they'd gone. Janie and I emerged from our room to assess the damage. We made Chris and Katie stay put. We found the fishbowl and all its contents strewn across the kitchen floor. Goldie lay still amongst the debris. I had hope, but Janie stiffened. She approached him and knelt down. "Watch the glass," she said, her voice flat.

"Is he dead?" I asked.

"I think so. I'm so sorry."

"It's okay."

She pinched Goldie's tail and peeled him off the floor. Wordless, I trailed her to the bathroom at the end of the hall. She settled on the edge of the tub, plopped the fish into the toilet, and pushed the lever. We watched him spiral down the bowl, sloshing about.

The tank sighed and quieted. A reverent hush fell over the room. The fish now gone, I could see it coming—the geyser that was Janie's sorrow. Her spine wilted and her face accordioned; her shoulders quaked. Then she sobbed. I stood there silent, ears throbbing, unsure what to do. She was sadder about Goldie than I was, and he was my fish. Finally, I reached out and laid my hand on her shoulder, like we used to do with Gramma when she went on a crying jag. There were so many more tears than I would have expected over a fish—even from Janie, who was tenderhearted. I watched her weep, a sad sort of weight settling onto my chest. Maybe it wasn't Goldie she was crying for after all.

The dreams began around the time I lost the goldfish. I would wake in a sweat at night. It was almost always the same: I would be poised on the dirt driveway of the Mason house looking up at its empty windows. At first, I would see nothing, but then a figure would begin to take shape somewhere inside. The figure would move toward a window— sometimes the kitchen, sometimes Aunty Patsy's old room, at times the front room. A face gradually emerged through the glare of the wavy glass. I always felt a bit frightened at first —intimidated by this vague apparition. In the dream, I was aware that the house was vacant; no one should be inside.

As the face pressed closer to the windowpane, I would realize it was Gramma. I would cry out and rush at the house. *Can you hear me, Gram?* I would shout. *Can I come in?* The words were bulky, sticky as molasses. I'd have to force them from my throat, my lips thick, my tongue like taffy. She wouldn't respond, only sit behind the glass gazing out with a sympathetic expression, helpless.

She knew. She was watching. Maybe she couldn't help, but she was still there—just as she'd promised. That was enough.

When I thought I might run up the porch steps and through the shed door, the image would vanish. I'd awake with a start, the room dark, my heart pounding. Vestiges of the dream lingered, a residue—cool, dewy. Gramma. The warmth of her essence might have faded, but it was comforting nonetheless.

Though Mom had grown more distant over these months, at times, she and Janie still confided in one another about their dreams. I kept mine to myself. I feared that if I told anyone, the dreams would stop. That was the last thing I wanted. Maybe I was Indian enough after all. Gram's spirit had come to me and with it, somehow, a message of hope.

OLD HAUNTS

It was the summer of 1975. Katie wore a white T-shirt with green lettering that read, "Almost Heaven. West Virginia," like the John Denver song. A lot of people had shirts like that in Parkersburg. Just across the Ohio River, people would add: "Because it's so close to Ohio."

Our family was alone in West Virginia now. Aunty Patsy and her family had left the state and were living in Indiana, where they ran a mom-and-pop shop. I had just graduated sixth grade, and we were leaving the state too—moving again, though I didn't know where. As we packed up, the only thing I knew was we would first go to Hubbell, but we wouldn't be staying. Mom didn't want to live in the UP anymore.

The morning we left for Michigan, I watched as Dad huffed and puffed, stuffing as much as he could in the trunk of our car. The Bel Air was gone now. We had a gold Ford LTD with a half-vinyl top. It was a fancy ride. It even had an aftermarket air conditioner, but Mom rarely let us use it. She said it burned too much gas, and Dad said the country was in an energy crisis. He said it was our responsibility to do what we could to conserve. Dad was patriotic that way, part of his soldier mentality. We'd ride with the car windows down instead, his cigarette ashes recirculating through the rear window, peppering our faces. *Your ashes are flying back in!* we'd yell to him. *Ah, quit your yappin'*, he'd say.

"Is it all gonna fit?" Mom asked. She was standing alongside the trunk, grimacing.

Dad was sweating in the Parkersburg sun. Tiny beads of perspiration had formed at his hairline where it swept back toward his freckled bald spot. "Dammit to hell," he said. He'd caught his hand on a sharp piece of metal and shook off the pain. "I hope the rear end doesn't drag." He lowered the trunk lid gently to test if it would close. "I think we got it. Better not hit any potholes."

I stepped up beside him, my green Barbie case clutched to my chest. "Here's this," I said. I had matured, but my Barbie case was still the first thing I grabbed wherever we went. Though I didn't play with the contents like I used to, I dared not lose the doll clothes Gram had given me.

"Oh, Tresie's Barbies." Mom forced a laugh. Moving day was always stressful.

Dad gave me a sour look but took them from me and stuffed some more. We'd often had to leave things behind when we moved, but they had never asked me to leave behind my Barbies.

In Hubbell, we stayed in the old house where Grandma Nelson still lived, along with my sister Anne, who had married and moved into the rambler. The morning after we arrived, the first call I made from Grandma Nelson's clunky black desk phone was to my cousin Lisa. I still had her number memorized.

Once, the year we first moved away, I'd received a Christmas card in the mail from Lisa. Inside was a note telling me that for Christmas, her mom said I could call them long distance. I could call collect, and they would pay the charges. She included her phone number, but I knew it by heart. We didn't have a phone at the time, so I asked a friend who lived nearby if I could use theirs for this purpose. They agreed, so on the evening Lisa had designated on the note, I threw on my jacket and ran the short distance to my friend's home. I didn't need boots. West Virginia didn't get much snow.

My friend lived behind us in a two-bedroom apartment with a low ceiling. The flat white building with turquoise trim was only steps from a creek, which habitually flooded in heavy rainfall. She and her little sister welcomed me in that evening and showed me to the phone. Their home sometimes smelled of the creek, of crawdads and wet twigs, but on that night it smelled of spaghetti. I envied them. Our money shortage had taken its toll on our menu.

Aunty Marjorie must have been waiting for my call that winter night, because she answered quickly.

"You have a collect call from Theresa," the operator said. "Will you accept the charges?"

"Yes, we will," my aunt said. After a quick hello, she handed the phone to Lisa. That brief holiday phone call was a bittersweet addition to my Christmas that year. It was my first Christmas without Gram, and somewhere inside I knew that if she had not died, I would have spent the remainder of my holiday with her in Mason. Lisa and I would have played with my new Quick Curl Barbie with the pink checked maxi dress and platinum blonde hair. Things would have been like they used to be.

Now I sat on Grandma Nelson's prickly brown couch and again dialed the Haikkinens' number. The rotary phone clicked and whirred with each digit until finally I heard ringing on the other end.

"Hello?" Aunty Marjorie had a sprightly energy about her and, much like her sisters, a melodic quality to her voice.

"Hi, Aunty Marjorie," I said. "This is Theresa."

"Trese!" She sounded genuinely pleased to hear from me. "You're up! Lisa will be so glad."

My cousin was raised like an only child, even though she had a much older brother whom I'd rarely seen. They called him Boots—another nickname—and he worked downstate. Gram had said he was a "state bull," a trooper for the state police. She had seemed proud when she said it.

Lisa's father, Uncle Jim, was the only relative I knew who actually still worked in a mine. By the seventies, the sole mining operation in the area was White Pine, about eighty miles southwest of Mason. My uncle must have worked the late shift, because I would often see him leave for work. He wore an engineer's jacket over drab work clothes and held a big lunch pail at his side. He'd plant his boots in the gravel alongside M-26 and a long, silver bus—the White Pine Express—would rumble up, hiss to a stop, and whisk him away. Mining provided an income for his family, but I think Uncle Jim's job took its toll on him. He suffered debilitating headaches and at times remained sequestered in his darkened room above the kitchen. There were days Lisa met me at the door with a finger to her lips. *Shh. We have to play outside*, she would whisper. *My dad has a headache.* On one occasion we forgot about Uncle Jim lying upstairs in the dark and burst through the front door with our outdoor voices. Before we even set foot past the kitchen, we heard him calling out over-head—*Lisa!*—in his Finnish accent with the tightly-tongued *L*. That was all he had to say. She flashed me a look, and both our mouths zipped.

Lisa was my second cousin and lived in the former home of her grandparents, who were my great-grandpar-ents. She told me once that Great-Grampa Otten had built their sunny, windowed front porch for his wife. It was the same porch where Lisa and I had played Barbies on summer evenings out of reach of mosquitos. Great-Gramma Otten had died in the mid-forties, long before I was born. She was sixty-one years old, the same age as her fourth-born daugh-ter, my gramma, when she passed. I heard Gramma talking about her once to someone. "Ma's legs were bad," she said.

"Big, open sores. Ulcers." Gram said they'd used maggots to clean her ma's wounds. The memory rattled her, and she hugged herself snug. "Ooh," she said with a shudder. Bad legs and a sunny front porch were about all I knew about Great-Gramma Otten.

I went to visit Lisa the day after I called her. She was only a few weeks older than me, and she, too, was showing signs of maturing. In the past, the first thing we would have done was break out the Barbies or the paper dolls, but on this visit she invited me to play baseball in the vacant lot beside Gramma's old house—the house itself was now occupied by a young couple with children. We met up on the makeshift ball field and chose teams. There seemed to be more kids in town now, only a few of whom I recognized. A lot of things had changed in Mason.

"Trese, you play outfield," Lisa said.

"I'm no good at catching," I confessed, but I trotted out beyond third base and waited. I'd never played in the vacant lot before. Gramma hadn't let us. It felt wrong to be standing in the middle of it. It felt like trouble. Behind me, the Mason house loomed. I was preoccupied by its shadow, its proximity, my longing for its rooms.

The game was going well. Someone had brought a bat and ball, but there weren't enough gloves, so we shared what we had. During one gloveless inning, a pop fly landed in my cupped hands, a satisfying catch that bloodied my finger.

"You okay?" Lisa called from across the lot.

"Yeah, I'm fine." I shook off the sting, as Dad had done in Parkersburg.

One of the boys living in Gram's house invited me in to get a bandage. I jumped at the opportunity. I trailed him up the porch steps, the *thunk* of my foot on the tread warm and familiar. My heart lurched and landed lopsided. I heard the *schlik* of the latch. Beyond lay the familiar smells of the shed, though there were traces of something new as well—the odor of family: father, mother, kids. The big door opened, and there stood Gram's kitchen: the same light, the same sound of voices reverberating against plaster, but the haze of Pall Malls was gone. The woman in the kitchen was thin and young, kind and pleasant. She asked me to have a seat at the table. I sat, wordless and spindly, my throat coiled.

"Goodness," she said, looking at my finger. "It's a small cut, but it sure did bleed, didn't it?"

I didn't speak as I watched her run water onto a cloth. She opened the drawer where Gram once kept her Scotch tape and writing pad, the one furthest from the flour bin. The swollen wood scraped against its frame as it always had, its rasp a glissando along my spine. She pulled something out and reached up into the cupboard with its familiar glass front. The shelves were lined with new items now. The ceramic Kewpie doll was gone. There was no green Sinclair dinosaur where Gram collected pennies for her grandkids. I once purchased a ninety-nine-cent pair of sandals at the IGA with pennies from that dinosaur. When Gram died, she'd been saving pennies for her grandson, Scott, Aunty Jean's youngest.

"We'll put a bandage on it," the lady said. "It'll be good as new."

I was speechless, addled. It was the first time I had been in Gram's house in years, the last place I sat with her, the last place I saw her alive. This house had belonged to *her*. It had been her home. It had been *my* home. Now, it was filled with strangers. As the lady approached, bandage dangling, my tongue unfurled. "This was my gramma's house," I blurted. I needed her to know. This was a sacred place.

She had applied the bandage and turned to discard the wrapper. "It was?" She looked around the room. "I bet it looks different now, eh?"

That was the last time I ever went inside the Mason house.

VAGABONDS

I sometimes wondered if I would have outgrown Gram eventually, the way Anne and Janie did when they became teenagers—the way I outgrew my parents when I turned thirteen. It began one spring day after school when I walked into our sparsely furnished townhome in a suburb of Lansing in Michigan's lower peninsula. That's where we'd settled after we left Parkersburg. Aunty Jean and her family were living in that area too, so we had a connection. We even stayed with them for a few weeks until Dad and Mom managed to gather the funds needed for a deposit on housing and first and last months' rent.

It was 1976, the year of our country's Bicentennial. School would be out soon. I hopped off the bus, walked the block home, and shuffled inside, lugging my baritone. I'd wanted to play the clarinet but gave up on that idea when I learned it cost money. I didn't even bother to ask Mom and Dad. The school offered free use of low-brass instruments—the only option for low-income students (we shared the mouthpieces too)—so I went with that. That's how badly I wanted to be in band.

Mom was standing in the doorway of the dining room that afternoon. She was dressed in an inexpensive yet fashionable pair of knit pants and a white blouse with wide swirls of purple and pearly buttons. Her hair was pinned up as it often was, teased at the top. She always reminded me of the mother in that song by Jeannie C. Riley, "Harper Valley PTA." Once I'd seen her in the living room of the Hubbell house dancing to that record, so maybe that's why. Behind her I noticed a map laid out on the makeshift dining table. There was a spark in her eye, an energy I'd learn to regard with caution. "Guess what, Trese!" she said. She didn't wait for me to respond. I'd become quite the sulky teen in recent months, so my family had given up on waiting. "We're moving! To Texas! The Rio Grande Valley!"

My chest sank. I was right not to trust that spark. *The Rio Grande Valley?* What the hell? (In seventh grade I'd learned it was cool to swear around my friends, but I kept it in my head at home.) "Texas?" I asked, my nose scrunched. "Why there?"

"It's supposed to be beautiful. There's even palm trees. We'll be close to the Gulf of Mexico!"

"But why?"

"Your Dad's gonna work there. For a top shop." A top shop was what Dad called a countertop and cabinet shop. Mom glowed with the prospect. She and Dad had been getting along a bit better in the past couple months, but I knew it was tentative. Luke cast a long shadow. Though I hadn't seen him since the trip to West Virginia, I knew he was still out there. Somewhere. His name popped up every now and again, aggravating things at home. I didn't know how Mom felt about it, but I was glad Dad persevered. Life with my parents could be tough, but I figured Janie was right. It was better if we stuck together.

"What about school?" I asked. I set my baritone down by the couch, the weight suddenly unbearable.

"Youse can finish school. We'll wait till it gets out to leave."

"But what about my friends?" I whined. "What about Penny?" Penny and I had developed a tight bond from the first day of school. We'd met while standing at the iguana terrarium in the corner of the classroom. I remember her dressed in an enviable pair of flares and a boho top. I had on a garage-sale plaid skirt from the sixties, a pair of yellow knee-highs with a pink rose print, and black and white saddle oxfords. I looked like a nerd, but she spoke to me anyway and swiftly became my best friend. She was funny and trustworthy and had brown hair the same as me—only hers was lighter. We were inseparable at school and often found ourselves in shared trouble. We'd ditched our first class together and served our first detention together too. She'd even stood sentry during my first real kiss. How would I survive without her?

"You can't tell anyone where we're moving," Mom said, looking stern now. "Not Penny. Not even school."

"Why?" I throbbed, outraged.

"That's just how it has to be. Once we get settled maybe

you can write your friends. But for now, you *can't say a word*."
Sometimes our moves were secrets, but we weren't told why.
I assumed it had something to do with bills.

Up until this point, our frequent relocations had seemed
like adventures. In the past, my sisters and brother were my
allies, my closest friends. If we were together, the moves
seemed—well, not good, but *okay*, since we had each other.
But now it was different. *I* was different. I had friends. I liked
my school. I had boyfriends, and *friends* who were boys, and
I was in the band! What about all that? I went upstairs to
my room and fell across my twin bed. I was the only one of
us kids who had a real bed that year. Katie, Chris, and Janie
slept on rollaways. I couldn't believe this was happening.
Who does this? Why did they pick *Texas*? What did they do,
throw a dart at the map?

We didn't have a telephone, so I couldn't call Penny. At
school the next day I immediately confided in her.

"You're *what*?" she said, her face red.

I pressed an index finger to my lips. "Shh. I can't tell anyone. And you can't either. My parents'll kill me." She'd seen
my parents in action when she stayed with us one weekend.
She probably figured I wasn't joking.

"Where to?" she whispered. She looked to be two blinks
shy of tears.

"I can't tell you that."

The white streets of Kingsville wavered in the heat. Humidity licked at our windows. We arrived midmorning, the LTD panting, a U-Haul trailer shackled to its hind end.

We'd been on the road a few days, stopping just short of the Rio Grande Valley. Dad and Mom had purchased a red-and-white nylon tent at Kmart before we left lower Michigan. It had served as our sleeping quarters along the route, its thick synthetic smell stuffing our nostrils at night. We'd stayed at campgrounds and state parks, Dad always sure to find a place with a pool or a swimming hole for us kids. We'd cooked our suppers over a fire and toasted marshmallows for dessert. We took frigid showers on an Arkansas morning after having our hamburgers eaten by an armadillo the night before.

"Think of it as a vacation," Dad had said. Oddly enough, it did feel that way at times.

We rolled slowly along blocks flanked by ground-level businesses until Dad spotted what he was looking for—a real estate agency. He pulled up along the curb, and he and Mom went inside. The car windows were fully open, so I snaked myself out and perched my backside on the door frame. I stretched my arms out across the rooftop; both the metal and the half-vinyl top were already skillets in the morning sun. I recoiled and slid back into the car.

"Is this where we're gonna live?" Chris asked, bright-eyed. He had flopped over the front seat and was looking up and down the street. He was a cute kid with a head like a pumpkin, big brown eyes, and a thick mop of brown hair.

"Who knows," I said.

"You didn't wanna move, did you, Theresa?" Katie asked. She was sitting in a stream of sunlight, cheeks of French vanilla, timid freckles dotting her nose. She looked sympathetic to my plight. "You're sad and you miss your friends." She had answered her own question; I didn't need to respond. Katie couldn't read books, so she'd learned to read people instead. It was her gift.

It was only Katie, Chris, and me now. The backseat felt almost ample. All three of us could stretch out whenever we wanted—one up in the rear window with the iridescent shells of dehydrated flies; one across the seat amidst the crumbs; and one in the floor well with the mass of toys and flattened sneakers, the drive shaft hump nestled beneath our knees.

We had lost Janie to her boyfriend. They'd met in Parkersburg, and though we had left there the year before, their relationship remained intact. Janie had graduated high school a week earlier in Michigan and immediately returned to Parkersburg. She planned to attend nursing school. Our family was dwindling. First Anne, who was back in the UP expecting her first baby. Now Janie. It had felt odd saying goodbye to her, all of us moving in different directions. I wasn't ready to be the oldest, and I didn't want to be. There were a lot of things I didn't want now, but it was all beyond my control.

Mom and Dad returned to the car in a short while. The real estate agent had set us up with a furnished rental opportunity in a mobile home park not far away. We drove the short distance and stopped at the office. It was a large park, with narrow, winding roads. The grounds were flat and decked with palm trees, many no taller than five feet—a total letdown. What was the big deal about dwarf palm trees? Surely Mom was disappointed too, but she didn't let on.

The manager showed us to the property, which had only just been vacated the day before. "You'll have to do the cleanup if you need it in a hurry," she told my parents as she popped the lock on the knob. She was pleasant and seemed apologetic about pawning the job off on us. "We haven't had time to clean it out yet." She swung the aluminum-clad door wide and extended an arm in welcome.

I sensed Mom's alarm the instant she hit the threshold. She hesitated with one foot on the metal stoop and then proceeded warily. I followed her—into a putrid cloud of stench. The room was steamy and reeked of skunk, the kind you'd find splattered along M-26. Greasy trash and dirty clothes dotted the interior. Whoever had just moved out had done so in a hurry. Shoes, boxes, and bedding were strewn from one end of the mobile home to the other. The kitchen looked like it hadn't been cleaned in weeks, perhaps months. Mom and I locked eyes, her arms stiff at her sides. Dad took one step inside and sent Katie and Chris skedaddling back to the Ford.

"Don't touch anything," Mom said, holding her nose.

"It is a mess in here." The park manager sighed and shook her head. She remained by the door.

Mom and I half tiptoed to the avocado-colored refrigerator. She opened it with two fingertips, peeked inside, and mock-gagged. "What is that?" she asked. Inside was a fish as long as a rolling pin. It was laid out on the top shelf on a sheet of white butcher paper. A spattering of splinter-sized, amber bugs clung to its gills. She shut the door quickly, her lips screwed up in disgust. "Ewww."

I laughed, astonished by the blight. I'd never seen a place so filthy. "That was gross."

"What was it?" Dad asked, bucket hat in hand, scratching his bald spot. Like the manager, he hadn't yet stepped away from the door. He didn't seem too interested in the place.

"You don't wanna know," Mom said.

After touring the three bedrooms and one bathroom, Mom decided we could handle the job. We didn't really have a choice. "I think we can have this cleaned out by bedtime," she said. She'd always been a workhorse, so I trusted her assessment. We gloved up and set to cleaning, a trusty bottle of bleach at our side.

Maybe it was the heat, or maybe the hormones. I wasn't sure which. Whatever was causing the problem, it wasn't getting any better.

"My head is so itchy!" I exclaimed as I came out of the olive-toned bathroom one afternoon. I'd just washed my hair *again* with the prettiest shampoo on the market: Clairol Herbal Essence. We rarely bought name-brand products, so this was a special treat. The emerald green solution smelled so heavenly, I couldn't get enough of it, but that wasn't the reason for my frequent shampooing. We'd been in Texas all of four months, and my scalp had been itching for at least one of them. I'd hoped shampoo was the answer, but it wasn't helping. "Mom, would you look at my head?"

"Your head is itchy?" she repeated. She was standing at the kitchen sink in soap-bubble gloves, Bermuda shorts, and a sleeveless top. She wore her pin-tucked face, the one that spoke of peculiarities. She grabbed a frayed dishtowel and wiped her hands. "Here. Sit down," She directed me to a gaudy, Mediterranean-style kitchen chair. I plopped down, pulled my hair up off my neck, and dropped my chin.

I heard her gasp.

"What?" I asked. "What is it?" My heart kicked. Mom didn't answer. "What do you see?"

"Oh my god," Mom said. "You're *infested* with 'em!"

"What?" I burst into tears. "What is it?"

"Stay right there!" she said, and ran out the front door. Terrified, I resorted to the familiar: I froze in the chair, afraid to move. She returned shortly with the neighbor lady. She was taller than Mom and thin, with what I recall as Frost & Tip hair. They stood behind me sucking air and manipulating my head like a joystick. I could smell Nair.

"Yep. It's head lice," the Frost & Tip lady confirmed. "Definitely." By this time my whole family had gathered. They stood in a wide circle observing the scene with horrified pity.

"Oh no," Mom said. "That's what I thought." She stomped her foot. "Those dirty *buggers*."

"What is that?" I asked, head still hanging, sobbing.

"Tiny bugs," the lady said loudly, as though I couldn't hear her because she was standing behind me. "They nest in your hair. You have to use a special shampoo and comb to get rid of 'em."

"Can I get that at the drug store, you think?" Mom asked.

"Oh, sure," she said. "But you better hurry." She lowered her voice. "I heard they once ate clear through to a woman's brain."

I was near hysterics. Mom patted my arm. "Don't be scared now, honey," she said over my bawling. She didn't seem fazed, but then again, it wasn't her head. "Mama'll get rid of 'em."

And so the battle of the head lice began.

Turned out I wasn't the only one in the family hosting those bugs, though I did have the worst case. For days Mom combed through our hair in search of sticky white eggs. It became an exhaustive nightly ritual as we worked to rid ourselves of the parasites that must have come with the mobile home's furnishings. "It's nit-pickin' time," she called out one night. She laughed until she had to cross her legs to keep from peeing—birthing us kids had been hard on her bladder. It was uncharacteristic of Mom to find humor in tragedy. I didn't find nits to be the least bit amusing. The incident scarred me for life—but I wasn't alone. Long ago, those bugs had left their mark on someone else. I was finally in on the secret: Mom had them when she was young. Uncle Blue had them too, though I never saw any bugs in his hair when I used to sift through it. There wouldn't have been any in mine either if we'd never left Michigan in the first place.

Not only did we battle the scourge of head lice in the Texas mobile home, we also contended with the worst infestation of cockroaches the exterminator had ever seen—both populations apparently cultivated by the previous tenant. In time, we conquered the bugs, but I was plagued by another curse: loneliness. I missed the friends I'd been cut off from in Michigan, and I didn't have the heart to make new ones in Texas. With any luck, we'd move again soon anyway. Isolation bred hope.

Then, somehow, Penny found me.

When summer passed without her hearing from me, she sent a letter to our former address in hopes it would be forwarded. We hadn't left a forwarding address to my knowledge, but heaven intervened. Within a few weeks, Penny's letter appeared in our Texas mailbox, a mummy bandaged in yellow postal service stickers.

"There's mail for you," Dad said, grinning. He tossed it in my lap where I sat reading a Trixie Belden book I'd borrowed from a neighbor.

I was stunned. I never received mail. I flipped the envelope over and read the return address. "Oh my god!" I squealed and leapt up. "It's Penny!" I tore at the edge, a thoroughbred galloping in my chest, and pulled out the neatly folded, handwritten pages. I ran to my bedroom to read them.

After much discussion, Mom and Dad agreed to let me answer her letter. "She needs to keep our address confidential," Dad said. "Do you think she can do that?"

"Yeah," I said. "I trust her. She's my best friend."

"Well, I hope she does," he said. That was the end of the discussion.

After that, Penny became my savior. We wrote once or twice a week. We wrote about rock groups like Queen and Aerosmith. We wrote about movies like *Carrie* and *Car Wash*—neither of which I had seen, but I wanted to. We wrote about Robby Benson and John Travolta. We wrote about middle school. But most of all, we wrote about boys. I didn't have a single friend in Texas, but I had the greatest pen pal in the world.

"I love those things!" I said to Dad. He was standing near a counter in cuffed work pants and an earth-tone polo shirt with a snag on the belly. His pack of Dorals formed a square in his thin chest pocket. I could see the red label through the fabric. Beneath his bucket hat, a flat, square pencil was tucked over his ear, which was peeling from a recent sunburn—Dad burned easily. He had just uncrated a colorful selection of Formica swatches, all neatly hung on a shiny ball chain.

"You like those, eh?" he said. "Here. Make yourself useful." He passed me a handful of loose swatches. "Add those to that ring, would ya?"

He had brought Katie, Chris, and me to downtown Kingsville to see his shop. He'd rented a small storefront off the main drag after other employment prospects fizzled out. Anne and her husband had loaned him the startup money. It was an old place with hazy windows and a broken-down sales counter in an untidy reception area. The back half was unfinished, with a cement floor and raw walls. It looked like his Hubbell woodshop before he turned it into our house. A fluorescent fixture whirred overhead, its light inadequate for the space. There was a table saw square in the center, a mound of salmon-colored shavings below. Dad hadn't worn his work boots that day; in the sawdust I could see a constellation of footprints from his canvas slip-ons. The room smelled like him, warm and woodsy, with a hint of Lectric Shave.

I threaded all the swatches onto the ring and organized the pamphlets and brochures from the carton marked "Haas Cabinet." Katie and Chris were busy playing tag. They giggled and argued; the tattling would start soon. I was surprised Dad was letting them run around inside. He usually put the kibosh on that real quick. They wanted me to join in, but I was too old for tag. I had more important things to do.

On a shelf near the front door a box had all but collapsed with age. It was dust laden, the color sapped by light and heat. It held a tangled hodgepodge of items left over from failed tenants. There was a black letterboard and a cache of white plastic letters. "Hey, look at this," I said to Dad as I sifted through the goods. "Can I use this stuff?"

He was preoccupied with his tools and didn't look up. "I don't care," he said. "Just don't hurt yourself."

I set immediately to work, digging for letters and placing them on the grooved board. When finished, I held it up, my chest puffed out with pride. "Look, Dad!"

He glanced up from his task. "Oh, yah," he said, smiling. "That looks real nice. Real nice." He seemed as proud as I. "Set it there in the window, why dontcha?"

I scurried over to the storefront, Katie and Chris trailing after me. I propped the letterboard in the window and went out onto the empty sidewalk to see how it looked.

It read:

Kingsville Kitchen and Top Shop

Proprietor: Derry Nelson

The colors of fall deepened and, along with the chrysanthemums, I bloomed. I was taller than Mom (not a phenomenal achievement), lanky in the legs and gangly in the arms. It seemed even my teeth had grown, accentuating my crooked incisors—a flaw I'd hardly noticed before. Puberty recast me. My skin protested the shift in hormones, as did my hair. Strands that once fell smooth and straight like Anne's now took on their own life. Frizz furled and kinked, and waves swelled asymmetrically (at times I blamed that on the head lice incident, but it could have been chlorine). A summer spent at the pool had toasted my skin to an apple-butter hue. I looked more like Mom, more Indian than I ever had—although, this close to the border, people often mistook me for Mexican.

At the time, Mexicans weren't called "Mexican" in our house. We referred to them as others did: "Spanish." I'd noticed not all the Spanish were held in favor in the area, though I had met several who seemed fine to me, some very kind even. Yet it was apparent many townspeople didn't care for them. They grumbled about the "illegals." (By the talk, I guessed that meant most were visitors—not bona fide citizens.) I heard them referred to in racial slurs. People joked about them "crossing the *reever*" and laughed about their accent and language. *¡Arriba, arriba!* they'd tease, mimicking Speedy Gonzales. I'd never given a disparaging thought to the Spanish before, but the more I heard these comments, the more I came to adopt them. By the time school started, I had developed quite an unhealthy opinion of the vast Spanish population, which seemed harmless when kept in my head—until I grew to suspect others thought I was Spanish myself. It began at school, where in one class it appeared to me the white kids had been seated in a cluster, while me and the Spanish kids filled in the field. Why wasn't I seated with the "American" kids? I was an American. Why was I lumped in with the Spanish—who didn't seem to want me there in the first place?

The seating chart became a daily source of contention. I was perplexed by the teacher's ignorance. Couldn't she tell the difference between an Indian and a Spaniard? I was a different shade of brown! Skin tone aside, there were other obvious differences between me and my seatmates. I noted some of them had wide, warm irises, lush lashes, and a deep espresso shade of hair. A few spoke Spanish on occasion (in particular, middle school insults), and others' words had the telltale accents of English as a second language. I didn't fit and that got me thinking. Maybe it didn't matter that I wasn't Spanish—it only mattered that I wasn't white. This perception hit me upside the head like a croquet mallet. I spent my days stewing about the perceived injustice, glaring at the teacher, scooting my desk out of alignment—making my own row. I was Chippewa. An *American Indian*, by god. If I was going to be discriminated against, it would be on my own terms.

Prejudice was a new development for me—both as the source and the target. I found it an ugly state of mind. I'd always felt like an island of sorts where my race was concerned, but I'd rarely judged or felt judged until I moved to Texas. I knew Mom had been discriminated against in the past—kids had made fun of her, people disliked her. My sisters told me they'd dealt with it, too, when they were in grade school. Back then, they weren't always known by name but rather as the "poor Indian kids." More than once, as they were walking home, they passed classmates on the playground overlooking Torch Lake. As the group played hopscotch or jumped rope, they'd pause their activity, become a gauntlet of sorts. "Look," the most vocal of the group said, sneering at them. "There's those poor Indian kids. We won't play with *them*." Those words doused my sisters' light right then and there. Neither Mom nor Grandma Woods could offer words of strength to make the bullying hurt less—perhaps they'd fallen victim to it so many times they'd come to believe it themselves, to accept it. Gramma Bertineau, on the other hand, had a thing or two to say about it. "You have nothing to be ashamed of," she said when Janie sat crying on the blue couch. "*They're* the ones who should be ashamed." She had really changed her tune through the years.

Either I was self-absorbed or just plain oblivious, but I don't remember anyone making disparaging remarks to me as a young child, the West Virginia incident aside. (There was one elderly woman in Hubbell who might have, but I steered clear of her.) In my heart, I carried my race like a scepter. I felt important—like history somehow lived on through *me*. Though I hadn't grown up a courageous child, in Texas I developed a backbone where my Indian was concerned. Such resolve was yet another example of the changes occurring within me. I was maturing, both emotionally and physically. I hardly recognized myself these days. There was little about my life that seemed familiar.

November would soon be upon us, and it was still warm in southern Texas. The air conditioner had not yet earned a sabbatical. It was midafternoon, and I was watching *The Gong Show* while lying on the ugly plaid couch. Everything was ugly in the mobile home, from the dark, scarred wall paneling to the green appliances. Even the smoked mirrors glued to the living room wall were hideous. It was a depressing place—or maybe it was just my frame of mind. At least it smelled better since Dad had removed the decaying mouse he discovered in the water heater closet. For that I was thankful.

At the corner of my eye, a reflection lit the tiled ceiling. I heard a car door out front and got up to peek out the narrow window in the dimpled door. Beside the five-foot palm tree stood Anne. She cradled her three-month-old daughter Beth in one arm; an overstuffed, quilted diaper bag swung from the other. She had flown down from the UP for a visit. I threw open the door. "You made it!"

"Cripes, it's still hot down here!" she said. She looked tired. Like Snow White, she was the fairest of us all, but her cottontail complexion had pinked with heat.

Dad was carrying her big, blue hard-sider suitcase. He and Mom had bought it for her when we first moved to West Virginia, so she could come visit us. "Christ, you should have been here a couple months ago," he said. "It was hot as hell."

Within a few days Anne had settled into our tight quarters. Mom picked up a used crib with a worn decal on the headboard of a bear cub sitting in a patch of yellow and blue flowers. She cleaned it all over with bleach and set it up in Chris's room. We spent our days ogling the baby. I hated to leave for school in the mornings; I pretty much hated school anyway. I didn't have any friends, and a few of the kids were flat out mean. Besides that, I had started my period, and I

184

wasn't good at managing it. There were times I would have to come home to change clothes, which worked out for me in the long run. The less time I had to spend at school the better.

One evening, I watched as Anne bathed the baby. She cupped Beth's head carefully with one hand while she dribbled warm water over her white, glossy skin. Beth kicked and arched and flapped her arms, her bright eyes blinking rapidly. "Ooh, who's getting excited?" Anne said, making turkey sounds into the folds of Beth's chin and neck. "Who's getting excited?" Anne liked to get the baby riled up at bath time.

"Seriously," I said when she had lifted Beth out of the water and laid her in a towel on the counter. "Why'd you come all the way down *here*?" I didn't care for our life in Texas. I couldn't imagine why anyone else would want to join us.

"Cause I wanted to visit," Anne said. "And I wanted you guys to see the baby." That didn't feel like the whole story, but I left it at that. She was a private person.

Since Anne didn't seem interested in returning to Hubbell any time soon, eventually her husband Bo joined us too. I heard mumblings of a rift between them which had been reconciled. Bo decided to look for work in Kingsville, as there was still little to be had in the UP. I loved having them with us. They were young and brought a playful vibe to the house. Unlike Dad and Mom, they liked to spend some of their money on fun. They were cool, too, and interested in the things I was interested in. They liked current music—David Bowie, Fleetwood Mac, the Steve Miller Band—and shared it with me. They'd see movies and buy fast food. Sometimes they'd take me with them. Once they even took me driving in their tuff blue and white Camaro along Padre Island, which was only an hour or so away. We rode along the shoreline, sunroof open, tires spinning in the sand, part of the "in" crowd. The air was brisk and I had on my navy zip-up hoodie with a thermal lining and a pair of OshKosh overalls Anne had given me—the only brand-name piece of clothing I owned. My hair was wild and stiff with the moist, salty breeze. The radio was playing. I wasn't a kid anymore. I was a teenager now, and teenagers got to do grown-up stuff like this. Anne and Bo made Texas almost fun.

Shortly before Christmas we gained yet another resident. Janie arrived from Parkersburg. Life with her boyfriend had not worked out as she'd imagined. Besides that, I think she felt left out since everyone else lived in Texas now.

"Are you sad you had to come back home?" I asked her one day.

"Nuh uh," she said. "I'm happy to be home." She and I were different in a lot of ways. That was definitely one of them.

Our numbers growing, we had to look for a larger place to accommodate us all. We couldn't stretch the mobile home any further. Dad and Mom didn't mind. They liked having everyone home—they must have been lonely too. They rented a nice rambler with an orange tree in the backyard.

We didn't have any furniture, but at least there was plenty of space to spread out. On moving day, we waved good riddance to the mobile home. Mom started giggling. "At least we left *that* place in a lot better shape than we found it," she said.

I was smushed in the back seat beneath a mound of laundry baskets, which had been stuffed full of everything but laundry. "I never wanna think about that place again as long as I live."

"You got my vote," Dad said.

The whole family was back together again, but it was temporary. Dad's new top shop was struggling. I should have made him a bigger sign. Rent on the new house took a chunk out of the budget, and there were a lot of mouths to feed, even though the other adults contributed their share. While the stress of a failing business and ensuing money worries heaped up, it was the troubling news Mom received one March day that really did us in.

Late one afternoon, several of us were watching TV in the den. We'd never had a house with a den before, so it was a novelty. Dad hadn't yet come home from the shop, but it was nearing suppertime, so he'd be walking in anytime. We'd all squeezed into the cozy room together, but only three of us could fit on the old, gently used Bridgewater sofa that had either been dragged home from a yard sale or left by a previous tenant. Everyone else sat on the carpeted floor. Mom was conspicuously absent from the group that afternoon. We soon saw why. She'd been in the kitchen sipping from the bottle of tequila Bo, Anne, and Janie brought back from a recent trip across the border to Matamoros, Mexico. Fully aware of its dangers, Janie had tucked it away, but somehow Mom had come upon it in a moment of weakness. She hadn't been drinking for a couple of months. Dad hadn't either, and he was usually the first to succumb. Things had been peaceful, but Mom must have been saving up.

She barreled into the den that afternoon midshow, gnarled as tight as a string of Christmas lights. She stopped just short of the couch, blocking our view of the television, seething like a bull at center ring. Her mood was black, her eyes two glowing coals. I could smell the bite of trouble on her breath. A sweet heat seeped through her pores—smooth and golden, delusive. My gut knotted. We'd all been laughing at the TV, the baby swinging in the corner of the room, but now our mouths zipped. My eyes darted to Anne and Anne's to Janie. We knew the risk of speaking. It could be anything—*Hello. What's for dinner?* Or, *What ya been drinkin', Ma?* When Mom came looking for a fight, it took only one wrong word to unleash the inevitable.

We all froze, waiting.

I don't recall who cast the pebble that brought on the meltdown that day, but I do remember the ripples that followed. Someone—maybe Katie—said *something* in that den and *kerplunk*. Mom leaned in, her words deliberate, her neck extended like a goose in a headwind. She threw down the challenge. "*What* did you say to me?" No one dared respond to the snarl, but it didn't matter. She was primed to ignite. If we didn't get to running real quick, we might be goners.

"Huh?" She was shrieking now. "What did you say?" Then she charged, arms flailing. Things just happened that way in our home. One always had to be on the ready.

Luckily the den had four exits, because we scattered in all directions like a palmful of jacks. All except Janie. She was tired of running. She turned and stood her ground, her voice thundering. "You knock it off!" she shouted from the den, where we'd all abandoned her to fight our fight. In the background I could hear the *tick-tick-tick* of the empty baby swing. "I've had enough of this!"

Beyond the wall, Mom was wailing now, spouting a diatribe none of us could decipher. Had we owned any furnishings I'm sure they would have been flying. But there were no chairs to toss here. No dishes to throw. All she could do was scream.

I huddled in the entry hall listening to the brawl, wondering how long it might go on, wondering if I should leave the house. Suddenly, there was a shift in emotion—a mutation in the hysteria. Mom's rage had sloughed off and exposed another layer. Some wound. Some desperation. I heard it in her pitch. I edged closer to the doorway. I wanted to know what was happening—to see what it was all about. I'd never taken much of an interest before. To seek shelter had always been my modus operandi, but on this day, with Janie running interference, I couldn't resist. Morbid curiosity sucked like a leech and around the corner I slunk. The sight was surreal—like a scene from a movie. Mom was laid out on the floor, reeling in some unleashed anguish, howling, raw and wild. She looked even smaller than usual, like a little girl. Like the child she was in the stories she told me—the ones about school, when white kids teased her and called her "squaw." I'd never been called a squaw—"Indian giver" was bad enough—but Mom had, plenty of times, and she *hated* the word. She hated the kids who used it. She told me she went after them, tried to make them pay. Her rage was mighty but her frame tiny. She'd sometimes wind up on the ground, kicking and screaming. Defeated. Yes. That is exactly how she looked there on our den floor. Her blouse was bunched up, her hair undone. A spray of coarse, black strands snaked across the bisque sculptured carpeting. Janie had straddled her and was yelling in her face. "Stop it, Mom! Shut up!" She slapped her once. Twice. I couldn't believe it. There were times I'd wished I could do that, but I never dreamed Janie would.

Mom carried on. She didn't seem to feel any of it—only what gnawed at her insides, whatever pain the tequila had fanned. Her eyes were closed, her chin high, her body writhing beneath Janie's weight. "He's married! He's married!" she finally cried. No names were mentioned, but I knew who she was talking about.

At last, Luke had thrown in the towel.

The tequila mishap brought an abrupt end to our stint in Texas. It was clear we'd all been there long enough. Maybe that's what Mom was trying to tell us—she just didn't know how. Within weeks we were all headed north again, though not all to the same destination.

"You're gonna love it here," Janie said.

It was June now, and I was standing at the end of the hall in the Hubbell house talking to her on the phone. I had returned to Hubbell with Anne and Bo when everyone left Texas in March. Janie, along with the rest of my family, had settled in Oklahoma.

Anne had surprised me in March with the offer to return to Michigan. "Trese, what do you think about coming up north with us for the rest of the school year?" she asked. "Up north" was what we called home. "It might be easier for you to finish the school year in Lake Linden. At least you'll know people."

I welcomed the chance to go up north. I certainly did not want to start an unfamiliar school with only three months left in the year. "Do you think Mom and Dad'll let me?" I asked, doubtful.

"Yeah." she said, winking. "I already asked."

I was grateful to Anne for bringing me back to Michigan with her, but it turned out to be a difficult adjustment. There was a vacant air to the area now, and a vacancy in me, too, like those once-lively motels outside Houghton.

One day, hoping to fill the void, I walked along the gravel shoulder the few miles to Mason. I was dressed in straight-leg jeans with a three-inch strip of floral fabric economically—though tastefully—added to the hem to increase their length. They had once belonged to Lisa. The brown suede chukka boots on my feet were a size and a half too big for me, but they were all I had. Anne had passed them down to me; I tripped a lot. I even fell down the stairs at school twice, once spraining my ankle. More of life's shoe conundrum.

I shuffled along the roadside in my too-big-but-cool boots, kicking grayscale stones left and right, pondering which ancestors might have mined them. I did that sometimes when I thought too much or when I was lonely. Every few feet I passed springs of snowmelt. They dribbled over blunt outcroppings of Jacobsville Sandstone, enhancing the ruddle in the rock. In early spring these rivulets gushed like geysers. I used to count them each Friday on the way to Gram's. Most of them would dry up soon; the snow was nearly gone.

I had just passed the skeleton of Quincy's Mill No. 1—its vast banks of windows riddled with broken glass, its brick and block remains scarred and crumbling—when beyond the bend the first slanted roof of Mason came into view. I stopped. Beside me, Torch Lake reflected the leaden sky, slung low like a cold, empty hammock. The blackened shell of a mining dredge listed at water's edge, its hull swallowed up in muck, its gantry rusted to burnt cinnamon. Across the narrow channel, the spring-brown, wooded lakeshore of Upper Point Mills loomed silent and uninhabited. Between that and the mill, I stood sandwiched in desolation. A car whooshed past on the highway—probably Houghton bound. A chill pricked. Why was I doing this? Ahead lay nothing familiar. Even Mason felt foreign now. What once was a welcoming sight—the sight I longed for, the sight I called home—had now become strange. Gram's house no longer belonged to me. I no longer belonged to Mason. I turned and headed back to Hubbell. I didn't know where I belonged anymore.

Over the past year, this feeling of not belonging had crept in and taken hold. I'd always relied on Gram to soothe me, but she no longer visited my dreams. Maybe that was the disconnect—she'd given up on me. I had changed a lot since she died. I'd even started smoking. I kept a pack of Marlboro Reds hidden outside beneath an old kitchen sink that was stacked against the rambler. Sometimes I bought Salems, too, like Mom did when she drank. I smoked with Hubbell kids in the woods or in the old shack up the hill, the one pieced together with discarded wood panels in a mix of finishes. It had a flat, water-stained roof that bowed under snow and a floor of pine needles and decaying leaves. It smelled of Marlboros, marijuana, and moss. It was built by the older kids, but sometimes we took possession, when they let us. We'd sit within its cold, damp walls and rag about our lives—none of us could brag—and listen to someone's boot-legged cassette of Nazareth's *Hair of the Dog*. I wasn't sure who I was supposed to be these days and didn't necessarily like who I'd become. I couldn't blame Gram if she didn't like me much either.

Now that school was out for the summer, I would soon join the rest of my family in Oklahoma. Dad had a friend there he'd known in the UP. They'd apprenticed together in a carpenter shop. He thought they might build cabinets.

"Where are we gonna live?" I asked Janie that day on the phone. They were currently living in an apartment but said they would be looking for a new place before school started.

"I think we're gonna find a house around here," she said. "Someplace close. Don't worry. You'll like it. I do." Janie was usually a good judge of our living conditions, but I'd grown weary of moving. I didn't look forward to starting at yet another school.

When I got old enough to be on my own, I'd live in the same place forever.

RED DIRT AND A REAL LIFE

Perhaps it was the threat of tornadoes that put the fear of God into Mom and Dad, or maybe it was simply a desire to do better. Whatever the case, when we moved to Oklahoma they stopped drinking. They both held jobs. Dad built cabinets for a local shop, and Mom worked as a nursing assistant at the Catholic hospital in downtown Oklahoma City. They went to work every day as scheduled. They came home each night, fixed supper, and watched the news. On Friday nights they sometimes took us out to eat. We'd pile into the new car, another Ford LTD, silver this time. Dad had grown to like Fords. We'd head to Der Dutchman, a local seafood favorite.

"Why'ntcha bring me an order of those frog legs to go, would ya?" Dad said to the server one night as we prepared to leave. Assured of his selection, he nodded and handed over his oversized menu. He liked fried frog legs for his midnight lunch.

"I think I'll take a few of these," Mom said, stocking her purse with packets of sugar and ketchup. She smelled

of Cachet by Prince Matchabelli—her Christmas cologne—
and had her hair pinned up as usual. "They're nice to have in
an emergency." She was not only a child of a reservation but
a child born on the receding edge of the Great Depression
as well.

"I might go to OU for college," I announced as Mom
fiddled with condiments. The University of Oklahoma had
piqued my interest the first winter of our arrival in the state.
It happened in January of 1978 while watching the Sooners
compete against the Arkansas Razorbacks in the Orange
Bowl. By fall of that year, my admiration had blossomed.
I hoped to one day be in the university's marching band.
Though our frequent moves and economic woes had derailed
my hopes of being a band student, with the help of a friend
I managed to make the drill team in high school. We per-
formed along with the marching band, snapping and twirling
red and white flags, sometimes a challenge in the Oklahoma
wind. After watching the Pride of Oklahoma, OU's marching band, perform on television during a halftime show, I
knew that was exactly where I wanted to be—marching right
alongside them in their flag corps.

It was our second year living in the same city, the same
house. Beguiled by stability, I began to make plans for the
future. Oklahoma was part of those plans. I loved living in
the state. I loved my school. I loved the red dirt in the baked
fields. I loved the people. I even unlearned past prejudice and
loved my "Spanish" friends—most of whom, I found, preferred the term "Mexican." Above all, I loved the fact that

there were many kids like me living in the area, kids with roots plucked by frequent relocations. I fit in.

We had settled in Del City, a suburb adjacent to Tinker Air Force Base, a sprawling installation with strong ties to the community. Life for those in the Air Force was always in flux, just like ours. Military families cycled through the area in two-year stints. Some less, some more. I felt a bond. I had an affection for Tinker as well. I loved the *warshh* as jet formations screamed past multiple times a day and the rumble of the AWACS planes, relatively new to the base. I felt a sense of security when fatigue-clad Tinker enlisted dropped their kids off at school or stood in line with me at the 7-Eleven, slurping cherry ICEEs. Tinker was like an American flag in the corner of a classroom. It commanded a quiet respect.

There was so much about Oklahoma I found endearing, even the spring tornado season. It was the culture of the state. It bonded us all. When there was a tornado warning, people gathered together. They'd hide in closets and in bathtubs, pillows and mattresses pulled tight overhead, sweating in the heat of adrenaline, waiting for the sound of an oncoming train. *Turn it to Gary England!* Mom would say of the television. Gary was the chief meteorologist for KWTV. He possessed a piquant Okie accent and a keen eye for storm cell rotation. He was regarded as the tornado authority in our home, which had become much like everyone else's home in the year and a half we'd lived there. I loved that too.

"OU?" Dad said that night at Der Dutchman. "Big school. What're you gonna do there?"

"Be on the drill team," I said. "The flags get to travel with the band. I could even get to go to the Orange Bowl."

"You're going to college like Janie?" Katie asked. Janie was taking her generals at the local junior college.

"I hope so," I said.

"You'll be a Sooner," Mom sang, her eyes twinkling.

"Would you be on TV?" Chris asked.

I shrugged. "Probably."

I couldn't wait.

It was my junior year in high school. My third year in the same spot. Well, not exactly the same spot. We had moved over the summer, but just to the house directly behind us. The new house was larger. I even had my own room. I slept in the two-car garage, which had been finished into a family room. It was separated from the rest of the house by a narrow laundry area, which had a rear exit I found especially convenient. My luck had finally come around.

"I call this room!" Chris said of the garage as we toured the place before we moved in.

"No," Mom said. "This is Theresa's room. She's the oldest." I *was* the oldest at home now. Janie had married and leased an apartment nearby.

"Are you kidding?" I asked. It was huge! And all mine?

Mom turned to Dad. "This'll be okay to sleep in, won't it?" she asked.

"Yah, she can sleep out here. It's all finished. She'll even have her own couch." There was a clean, sturdy couch dressed in a blue and white floral brocade positioned against a dark-paneled wall. The previous tenants had left it behind.

When we moved in, my luck continued. I managed to score a double bed with a foam mattress. I have no idea how that fell into my grasp. Some of our belongings from the Hubbell house had caught up to us as well in the few years we'd lived in Oklahoma. I had Gram's antique bureau with the pretty ring pulls—the one that once held her starched handkerchief collection. Her chestnut acoustic, a vintage parlor guitar bequeathed to me after her death, stood propped in a corner of my room. I even had the little blue hankie that belonged to Grampa Bertineau. I stored it in a miniature cedar chest with a broken clasp. I stashed all my little treasures in there, mostly things Gram had given me. She'd even given me the chest itself one cleaning day long ago.

I didn't have a closet in my room, but I had two cardboard clothing wardrobes where I hung my things. My red satin drill team uniform and white vinyl knee-high boots were tucked away in one of them. It was spring, and marching season was long over. I'd need a new uniform my senior year, but hopefully the boots could be used again, though they were starting to flake a bit around the zipper. I had to pay for everything myself, so I tried to take care of my things. On the floor next to the wardrobes, my green Barbie case sat collecting dust. Katie sometimes played with them if I was there to supervise, but I wouldn't let her take them out of my room. It was a strict rule. They were still precious to me. Maybe even more so after all these years.

I was sitting on my couch late one afternoon talking on my touch-tone desk phone. I'd convinced Mom and Dad to let me get it when we moved in, complete with my own number. I worked at Burger King and paid the bill myself. (Dad didn't mind that I had my own phone line, though he didn't like that he could hear it ringing through the vent late at night when I wasn't home.) I was chatting with Ben, the on-again, off-again love of my teen life. Ben and I made for better friends, which was what we were originally. We were laughing about *Speed Racer*, which I was watching on the portable television I had received for Christmas that year, when my bedroom door flew open. Chris rushed in. "We need to come in here," he said, pupils dilated, cheeks flushed.

Katie was close on his heels, rattled with fear. "Dad and Mom are fightin'," she said. She had our mother's eyes, crisp black droplets in pools of white, oil on snow.

Chris waved her in and shut the door behind them.

"I'll call ya back," I said into the receiver and hung up. "What's going on?"

Chris shrugged, trying to regain his cool. He was eleven but wise beyond his years. "They just started fighting."

I felt like an orange peel, my heart shriveled around the edges. Maybe it wasn't what they thought. Maybe they'd overreacted. Chris paced the cream-colored linoleum while

Katie listened at the door. I could see her reflection in its full-length mirror, stark and afraid, vigilant. She reminded me of a fallout shelter sign. I homed in on the sounds beyond my walls. My room was separate enough that I rarely heard a thing from the house, but now I did—echoes of a past I thought we'd outrun, outsmarted. It had found us, caught up to us. I'd been foolish to place faith in stability. I knew that now as I listened to our lives being shredded, the violent dismantling clawing through the aluminum ductwork. I heard the screams and shouts. I heard the battering of walls and furniture. The louvered register quivered as it held it all captive. It had been a long time since I'd heard those sounds, but my reaction was the same. Panic. The tremble surged upward through my legs, my gut, my shoulders, then into my teeth. They clattered as though I stood at the Hubbell bus stop on a February morning. I felt seven again. I wanted Anne or Janie. I wanted to run to the farthest room away. I wanted Anne's room, but I realized my room was Anne's room. *I* was Anne now.

Katie hung on my every breath waiting for guidance. She and Chris had come to *me*—the oldest. I tried to rein in my fear. "They haven't been fighting," I said. There was still a part of me in denial, a part in disbelief. "Are they drinking again?"

"They've been fighting, Theresa," Katie said, head bobbing, consonants dropping, *V*s slurring to *B*s. Her speech was commanded by her emotional state, much like my intestines. "When you're not home."

I was often gone these days, working or out with friends. I had noticed when a window got broken recently. Dad said a lawn chair had blown against it in a storm, but he didn't look me in the eye as he said it. I was aware of a shift in their mood too. They didn't eat out anymore on Friday nights. There was unrest at Dad's work. They seemed more irritable, less open. I had not, however, noticed any signs of alcohol. How did I miss it? There must have been cans or bottles *somewhere*.

The clamor in the vent had moved around to the kitchen. I could hear it through the laundry room now. It was too late to get out the back door. They would see us, and we dared not draw that wrath upon ourselves. "Let's go," I said. I went to my window, which overlooked the driveway and the LTD parked directly out front. I hoisted the aluminum sash and popped out the screen. In broad daylight, along a well-travelled street, Katie, Chris, and I squeezed through the small opening and out onto the sun-warmed, silver hood of the Ford.

Another funeral. It was the first I'd attended since Gramma's. Dad's buddy—the one he apprenticed with in his youth and the reason we'd moved to Oklahoma—had passed away after a lengthy illness. I didn't know the man well and hadn't seen him in a couple of years myself, but I could see our attendance as a family was important to Dad, so I didn't balk at joining them.

We filed into the Oklahoma City funeral home dressed in our church clothes. Mom smelled of Aqua Net and Avon; Katie's feisty hair had not yielded to the brush, and Chris's brown polyester pants barely reached the tops of his ankles. Dad had forsaken his trusty moc toe work boots for a pair of dark, matte oxfords with a creak in the leather. We followed him down the aisle, fluorescent tubes humming overhead, the *swoosh swoosh* of our fabrics noticeable in the hush of the chapel. Other attendees gazed at us, seeking a distraction, another focal point, something other than death. When we neared the front, Dad turned and waited, shoulders squared, as we all silently funneled, out of customary order, into our upholstered seats. Mom went first, then Katie, Chris, me, and finally Dad. He filled the space beside me with a glum warmth. It was odd sitting beside him, elbow to elbow. That was usually Mom's place.

We waited for the service to begin, reverent in the stillness, listening to the sporadic sniffling of family members across the aisle. Chris heaved an occasional sigh. Mom whispered some directive to Katie. Dad sat motionless, his knees parted, fingers laced, staring straight ahead. He was ransacked inside. I could tell as I watched him. His face was drawn, his pecan eyes dewy and desolate. He looked as lost as a penny in a storm drain. I looked down at his hands. At the loops of white hair sprouting from his freckled fingers, at the *U*-shaped blush of his nails, the ruddiness of his skin, his riprap knuckles. Dad had the hands of a carpenter, square, sturdy. He had fatherly hands. When I was little, I used to imagine he had hands like Jesus.

I knew he was hurting. I wanted to reach out to him, to take his hand, to comfort him. I stiffened, trying to build up my nerve. We rarely showed affection for one another these days. Our relationship had soured. I was angry with him—with both my parents. I loved Dad, but he had let me down. Every twelve-pack of beer he lugged home, every top he popped, was another petal plucked from the bloom until all that remained of my respect was a bald pistil and an anemic stem. Maybe it was the teen in me. Or perhaps it was the alcoholic in him. The combination had built a barrier between us.

Precious seconds ticked by and still I could not reach out. My arm was numb with conflict. How might he react? Would he reject my condolence? Our family didn't do emotion like others. With us it was feast or famine. It felt out of place, holding Dad's hand in his sorrow. Yet I wanted to. I needed to.

Suddenly, he raised a palm to his dry lips, released a restrained cough. He readjusted himself atop his cushioned seat, picked up a pocket-size pamphlet, and began reading.

Maybe that was for the best.

"Do you wanna come up north with us for the Fourth?" Anne asked. She was in Oklahoma visiting for a couple weeks but planned to return home before the Fourth of July.

It was the summer of 1980 and I was entering my senior year of high school. We were standing in my garage-turned-bedroom while I dressed for a date. Anne had loaned me her powder-blue Swiss-dot blouse to go with my blue seed-stitch tube top. I was wearing a pair of pleated denim trousers with suspenders and blue canvas flats. My hair was permed in ringlets, like Barbra Streisand on her *Wet* album. Everyone wanted a curly perm that summer. Even the guys. Though my hair now curled on its own, a perm offered more control. It gave me a defined style. I didn't look like Arlo Guthrie anymore.

I was going out dancing that night with someone I'd recently met from Tinker. He was nineteen, tall and commanding, with a knack for getting me into dance venues underage. Ben and I had painfully called it quits—again. Mom wasn't too pleased with me dating what she called "an older guy," but I didn't think much of our two-year age difference.

"I'd love to go home for the Fourth," I said to Anne that night. I never passed on a chance to spend the Fourth up north, and I could use a little time away. Spring had been rocky with Mom and Dad. They had returned to their drinking and money was scarce. I couldn't tell which had come first—the money troubles or the beer. Either way, it was the same result. Things had quieted down in recent weeks, though—a hopeful sign. It felt safe to leave the younger kids.

Janie wasn't far away. They knew they could come to my room if they needed to, and they knew how to get out safely too. "I'll see if I can get off work."

It was dusk when I walked into the Hubbell house at the end of the long hall. The Fourth of July had passed. I would be returning to Oklahoma before long. Anne was standing near the kitchen talking on the wall phone. She turned her back to me as I came in. I could hear her muttering to whomever was on the other end of the line. "Mm hmm. Mmm. Mm hmm." As I passed by, she held the receiver out with a stiff arm. "Mom wants to talk to you," she said. "Be ready." Her lips flatlined, underscoring her words.

I frowned and took the receiver. "Hello?"

"Hi, Trese," Mom said, her voice tenuous.

"Hi. What's up?"

She drew a deep breath, audible over twelve hundred miles. "I got some news to tell you."

I waited. The hair on the back of my neck rose. Gramma used to say hers did that too—right before lightning struck.

"We're moving," Mom said. She hesitated. I was mute, orphaned by my voice. "We're gonna move back to Michigan!" She tried to sell it. "We're gonna live in Hubbell again! You don't even have to come back here. We'll pack your stuff."

I stood stiff, my body sapped of energy, a corpse attached to a phone receiver. I couldn't even ask why we were moving. I didn't need to—I knew.

"Trese?" Mom asked.

Why was I so afraid to speak? I knew I couldn't change their plans, but I had to fight for myself. I needed to say good-bye to Oklahoma. I wanted to see my friends one last time. I wanted a proper ending. Gears lurched and words slogged to the surface as a long-dormant assembly line squeaked back into production. I heard my voice, thin and wavering. "No," I said. "I'm coming home. I wanna pack my own stuff."

It was a start.

Spirits appeared the night Mom called. Unwelcome ones. Dark ones. They slithered into my dreams. They came as the troubled souls of my parents. I dreamt I could hear them fighting beyond my bedroom door in the Hubbell house. I dared to leave my room and went out into the kitchen to confront them. They stood there, warped, cold, and black with evil, and glared at me as I approached. On the floor at their feet lay my parents as well, another set—the *good* set—dismembered, bloodied, and lifeless. I screamed and ran from the room.

I awoke tearful and terrified. The sun was up. I shared a room with Beth, my young niece, but her bed was empty. I was alone.

Anne opened the door to the bedroom. "What's wrong?" she asked. I must have called out in my sleep. "Are you okay?"

I was foggy and dazed. My trunk quivered. Anne sat down at the edge of my bed. I laid my head on her lap, wrapped my arms around her hips, and held tightly to her.

A day or so later, I was on a bus to Oklahoma City.

I'd caught a virus on the bus ride home, a chest cold or maybe bronchitis. I was sure my immunity had been knocked out of commission by the shock of the move. I had a cough and a low-grade fever. It was a Saturday afternoon and I lay miserable on the couch in the living room, unwilling to move, unable to cope. My bed was gone. It was outside in the driveway. Dad had gone crazy selling half the house in a yard sale, downsizing our lives to the dimensions of a U-Haul trailer. Both my parents had gone crazy.

"Hey," Dad said to Mom. He had just come in through the front door and was standing in the living room. "I sold that bureau in Theresa's room. Some woman offered me ten bucks. I thought it best to get rid of it. We can't haul that thing."

"Oh," Mom said. She was sitting on the love seat taking a lunch break. She shrugged. "Okay."

Bile surged. I wanted to scream. I wanted to pound at him for selling off Gramma's precious dresser—*my* dresser—but I had never risen against my parents in anger, except in my dreams. I lacked Janie's courage. Instead, I sprang off the couch and ran into my bedroom. I heard my parents behind me.

"What the hell's gotten into her?" Dad asked.

"I don't know," Mom said.

My room was nearly empty now, but my desk phone was still connected, sitting on the floor. The blue floral couch was still there as well. I dialed Ben's number. We were just friends now.

I heard his voice on the other end of the line. "Hello?"

"Can you come here?" I asked. "I need some help."

"Sure," he said, sounding confused. "I'll be there in a few minutes."

Once he arrived, he agreed to my request. He would store a few of my possessions at his house until I returned to retrieve them. Somehow, I would get back—hopefully, for college. We hastily loaded them into his car: my miniature cedar box, Gram's guitar, my green Barbie case, and a crate with my Shaun Cassidy collection.

Curbside, he handed me a mixtape for the ride to Michigan. I had a portable cassette player and a stash of batteries for the road. "It's got the new Christopher Cross," he said. "'Sailing.'"

"Thanks. I'll need it." I couldn't cry, but I wanted to.

"You'll be back," he said, wrapping his arms around me. I couldn't tell if he embraced me in solace or farewell. I hugged him back, but I didn't feel it. I had already detached—goodbye was too painful. "One year," he said into my hair. "It'll go fast." He slid into his black bucket seat and I closed the door behind him. I stood barefoot in the Bermuda grass and watched as he drove away, my life's treasures fading off in the back of an orange Oldsmobile.

LOST TREASURES

Thirty-eight hours with Greyhound—that's what it took to get back. I'd become a near permanent fixture of the bus. The upholstered seat had bonded with my backside, and a sweet, chemical latrine odor was embedded in my hair and clothes. But I didn't mind. I was almost home. The bus wheezed to an angled stop at the crumbling curb, and the driver reached for his handset. I heard his voice over the PA system. "Oklahoma City," he said, barely audible. My heart leapt as though he had shouted the words from the rooftop.

Two months after leaving Oklahoma with my wayward parents, I was back to live with Jane and her husband Andrew. They waited across the busy downtown street beside their Olds Starfire—physical opposites, Andrew towering above Jane like an Italian cypress. He was a friendly guy of Caddo-Comanche-Mexican descent who possessed the same sense of humor I'd seen in my uncles. It seemed a lot of Indians viewed life through the lens of humor. I interpreted it as a survival skill.

As I emerged from the coach, they crossed to greet me.

We hugged and collected my trunk. It was light blue with a large silver hasp, like one Mom used to have. I sniffed at my armpits as we headed toward the car. "I smell," I said. I was wearing my favorite shirt—a red-and-white baseball tee from the local rock station, KATT-FM. It was wise to look a little edgy on the bus, where there were always unsavory characters.

"Did you have any trouble?" Jane asked. She looked tired. She was a nursing student now, and Andrew was a lab tech at a local hospital. He looked tired too. Maybe marriage had that effect.

The two had met as students at Oscar Rose Junior College, where Jane served on the board of the Indian Student Club and did her work study in the Office of Indian Student Services. There were a lot of Indians in Oklahoma. The Indian Removal Act of 1830 drove several tribes from the southeastern United States into a newly designated "Indian Territory" along what became known as the "Trail of Tears." I'd learned about it in my ninth-grade Oklahoma history class. As entire tribes were forcibly marched across the country, thousands fell victim to disease and starvation. Those that survived managed to reestablish themselves in the new land—what would become the state of Oklahoma. Other tribes were indigenous to the area, and still more converged upon it as they were driven from their lands in other parts of the country. That's why, nearly 150 years later, there was so much diversity in the Indian population across the state.

Janie received an education grant through our tribe, the Keweenaw Bay Indian Community. Through her work at the college she developed a large network of friends. They called themselves "Skins." The college, however, preferred to call them "Native Americans," which had suddenly become the politically correct term. In our family, we still called ourselves Indians, though sometimes I wondered if we weren't supposed to. Andrew called himself an Indian too. To me, he was the true Western kind with straight, black hair (shorn short), jet eyes, and skin of rich sienna. Growing up, I'd never seen an Indian of that skin tone in person. All the ones I knew were taupe.

When we reached the car, Andrew hoisted the hatchback and tucked my baggage in the rear. I stood for a moment and arched my back, my face in the breeze. Like the smell of Pall Malls in Gram's house when I was young, the hot, dry wind of Oklahoma now signified home for me.

"You made it in time for the state fair," Janie said.

"I know! I might go with Ben and them tomorrow. Is that okay?"

"Fine with me."

I climbed into the cramped back seat and admired the familiar sights along the drive back to the apartment: the salt-white cube of the Myriad Convention Center where I'd attended so many concerts; the pretzeled Interstates 40 and 35, which served as the crossroads of the country; the thirsty red riverbed of the North Canadian. It all looked beautiful to me. I could hardly believe I was back. I could hardly believe Mom had allowed it. I knew it was hard for her to let me return. She didn't want me to leave Michigan—or her, perhaps—but surprisingly she'd agreed one evening before supper.

"What's wrong with you?" she asked me that night. She had grown impatient with my mood. It was Wednesday. She was standing near the stove in the rambler of the Hubbell house.

I slept in Anne's old room then—I wouldn't claim it as my own—and came downstairs to eat, eyes red, face puffy. The lavender walls weren't cutting it. I sat at the table, my forehead supported by my tented forearms. I had spent a lot of time in tears since we left Oklahoma.

Mom waited for my answer, but I couldn't speak. Instead, I sobbed. Katie and Chris sat motionless at their sides of the table. "What's the matter?" she asked again, more gently this time.

"I wanna go back to Oklahoma," I heaved. The words fled in leaps. I gulped for air. It was out there now.

She was silent for a bit, a long spoon in hand. Dad stood listening on his worn patch of linoleum at the sink, the place he always stood. He didn't intervene. Mom came to the table and stood across from me. I looked up at her through the blur. I could taste my pain, like baking soda and warm water. It pooled in the corners of my lips. "Where would you live?" she asked.

"With Janie." I had called Jane earlier in the week to ask if I could come live with her. I planned to run away. I had stashed ten dollars for food, and Jane had reluctantly agreed to pay for my bus ticket. All I needed were the guts to follow through.

Mom seemed tangled in her thoughts. Her gaze fell away, to the faded flecks on the floor, to the years gone by, to the ones still to come. "You don't like it here?"

"No." I couldn't tell her how much I missed Oklahoma. I couldn't tell her how much I missed my *life*.

She sighed, then shrugged. "I guess if you wanna go, go."

"I can? Really?" I didn't trust her words. I didn't trust her.

"I guess." She had eased herself onto a chair. "When would you leave?"

My suitcase was already packed, hidden in the back of Anne's closet. "Friday."

I had been back in Del City for a week or so. I was reenrolled at the high school and had spent a hot, dusty day at the state fair with Ben and a few other friends. It was Ben's treat—I was completely broke. We had stayed well into the evening, when the dirt cooled and settled and the carnies cajoled. We strolled the lanes of the midway as metal cages spun overhead, coins and flip-flops fell from the heavens, and the drone of weary motors drowned out the screams. We shared funnel cakes and elephant ears doused with powdered sugar. We played ring toss and water pistol games and watched the Space Tower—Oklahoma City's version of Seattle's Space

Needle—rise and fall in the cantaloupe sunset. The state fair was a perfect way to celebrate my return, but it was the simplicity of shared laughter that renewed me.

Though I hadn't missed the fair that year, I had missed out on drill team. I'd known that would be the case when I packed my trunk before I left Michigan. I had stashed my white knee-high boots in a box in the Hubbell house attic and left my old uniform hanging in Anne's closet. There was no need for them now. When I attended my first home game as a Del City High School senior, I sat in the stands and watched the marching band perform their pregame and halftime shows without me. Life had become a series of holes—some of which could never be filled.

It was a Saturday afternoon when I borrowed Janie's strawberry-red stick shift. I had only recently learned to drive it, and the clutch was still a challenge. "I hope I can make it there!" I said, laughing. I planned to go see Ben.

"Just go slow," she said. "And don't stop on an incline." I wasn't too worried about that. Del City was relatively flat.

I drove the short distance to Ben's house, surging and stalling a time or two. He lived in a one-and-a-half-story bungalow beyond the high school, just a few miles away. When I arrived, he met me at the door. He knew why I had come.

"Thanks for keeping my stuff," I said. "I was so scared Dad would get rid of it."

"No problem," he said. "You know I wouldn't want that to happen to you."

I followed him through the living and dining area, where I waited at the base of the staircase that led to the upper floor. I watched as he climbed the narrow steps. He was wearing cowboy boots, his long legs sheathed in denim. I'd met him as a boy, but he was becoming a man. He ducked a bit in the stairwell, then disappeared from view at the top. Within moments he reappeared, Gram's guitar in hand. I climbed halfway up the stairs and took it from him. "There it is!" I said. I smiled at the warmth of Gram's spirit in my palms, at her DNA embedded in the fretboard. He retrieved the other items and we hauled them out to the car. Relief settled over me; all my pieces were back in place. I thanked him again, tooted the horn in parting, and off I lurched in a labored first gear. In my rearview mirror, I saw Ben laughing.

Several days later, I was lying on a mattress in the walk-in closet of the apartment's master bedroom, which was where I slept. Janie and her husband had a one-bedroom unit, so the closet had become my temporary sleeping quarters. We were going to look for a two-bedroom place soon. I had my job back at the Burger King and would pay the difference in rent. Janie was still a student, so they were a one-income household.

I sifted through my miniature cedar chest that I'd picked up at Ben's, reminiscing. I decided to go through my Barbie case too. I couldn't remember the last time I'd opened it. When I'd handed my things to Ben a few months before, I was in such a state I didn't have time to give it all a proper goodbye. I unzipped the lid and folded it over.

I stared, shocked.

Inside was a tattered mess. Only a couple of dolls and a scattered mishmash of clothing and accessories remained.

Gram's handmade Barbie clothes were all but gone.

APRICOT KISSES

H is name was Noah.

It was the winter of 1983. We wound through the streets of south Oklahoma City in his blue and silver Chevy Silverado. Hall & Oates was playing on cassette—the *H2O* album. The streetlights strobed across his face as I watched him drive and point out landmarks along the route. I'd only known him a few days, but I felt perfectly safe.

"So, whenever you come over," he said, "all you have to do is look for Blackwelder. My house is easy to find."

No sociopath would draw me a map to his house. Clearly, I had nothing to fear.

We'd met at Graham Central Station. It was a Monday— rock 'n' roll night at the customarily country and western club. I noticed him across the bar: green eyes placid, framed by acetate aviators with teardrop lenses, storm windows to his soul. I'd always been attracted to men with glasses. They possessed the draw of intellect.

I waited for him to approach, to ask me to dance, but he didn't. When the DJ played the Gap Band's "You

Dropped a Bomb on Me," I decided to take a chance. I slid off my barstool and confidently marched over to him. He looked somewhat alarmed as a I approached—not a good sign.

"Would you like to dance with me?" I asked, smiling.

His chin dipped. "I'm sorry," he said. "I think I'm gonna sit this one out. I don't care for this song at all."

My ego deflated. "Oh," I said. "Okay. Well, thanks anyway." I turned to walk away, but he stopped me.

"Another song?" he asked. He grinned beneath his mustache, handsome. He wore a crisp white western-cut shirt with mother-of-pearl snaps and sharp points on the yoke. His feet were gloved in tan, suede western boots, the leather bruised and worn thin in places—a second skin—with arrowed toes and sloped heels. I thought he might be a cowboy. Like Indians, Oklahoma had a *lot* of cowboys. "Really. Another song," he said. "Come back again."

I left him then. Come back again? Ha! I returned to my barstool beside my girlfriend, where I nursed my buck-a-drink-till-ten rum and Coke and smoked a Benson & Hedges. I tried to avoid looking his way, but I liked him. It was something in his eyes.

A few records later, the DJ eased the needle to an album. The beat jounced against my chest. My eardrums quivered as ice in my tumbler jiggled. "Billie Jean" pulsed through the nightclub. Lights spun as droves of eager revelers abandoned their barstools. They filed out onto the dance floor, hands joined, couples tethered together like paper doll chains. I had reached behind me to stub out my cigarette in a plastic ash-tray when I heard his voice.

"Would you care to dance?"

I turned to find myself boot to boot with the green-eyed cowboy. In my experience, Okies generally had one of two accents. There was the quick-tongued pertness, like Gary England's from Channel 9. Then there was a low, slow drawl, like that of the cowboy standing before me. He donned a Sam Elliott grin, his head cocked slightly to one side.

"Oh. So you like *this* song," I said.

He nodded. I nodded.

And off we strolled onto the largest dance floor in Oklahoma City.

It was late May; summer was underway. Noah and I had returned from a long weekend camping with friends at Beavers Bend State Park in the southeastern part of Oklahoma. Beavers Bend was my favorite state park, tucked within the protected boundaries of the Ouachita National Forest. The area reminded me so much of the UP, with its mature stands of pine and hardwoods, ancient trunks rising up from fallen foliage, trails meandering through rust-colored beds of pine needle. Unlike those of central Oklahoma, the Ouachita's lakes, rivers, and streams were unmuddied, and its unique geological outcroppings added a textural richness to the landscape. It was a fishermen's haven, a campers' dream, just like the Keweenaw. I'd heard many say Oklahoma was a vast land of flat terrain, an unchanging view, a flyover state, but I'd come to know it as so much more.

I had taken Tuesday as a vacation day, but Noah returned to work that morning. I'd learned he wasn't a cowboy after all. He didn't ride horses or rope steers but pulled casing and plugged oil and gas wells instead—just as impressive, to me. He worked in the oilfield with a team of friends his age, all adept at the art of workplace safety in an often risky occupation. No, he didn't work cattle, but he was all Okie nonetheless—I liked that anchor in him.

I was at his place packing up my things, preparing to head back to my apartment. I was alone there, but apprehension nibbled: *Was I really alone? Was there someone else here with me now?* It had come to my attention over the weekend that my monthly visitor was late—my moon time, as Janie would call it. As a Catholic, I tracked my rhythm by habit, but springtime had been a blur with work and a new relationship in bloom. I'd neglected my duties. When the calendar pointed out my error, I'd paused and assessed my status. There were no usual signs of pending menstruation. No cramps. No fullness. It felt like the middle of my cycle, not at all the end. My gut pulled in on itself. There was a tingling in my spine, my ribcage, my limbs, an unfamiliar awareness of the space low in my trunk. This unease had ushered me the night before to the nearest Eckerd Pharmacy, where I purchased one of those early pregnancy tests that were fairly new on the market. The light blue cardboard cube with a daisy on the label now sat like a centerpiece on the lacquered wire spool that served as Noah's cocktail table, where I laid it after reading the instructions. I could sense his discomfort with it the moment I set it down—how he avoided looking directly at it, how he gently nudged it away when we sat down with our takeout, as if acknowledging the blue box might imply he welcomed the prospect within, might somehow initiate a positive result. I understood his concern. Though the possibility of a life within me fanned a certain sense of biological wonder and of reaching maturity, was either of us ready? I was so young, and we'd only just met months before.

"When do you take it?" he asked of the test before he left in the morning. "How long before you know?"

"I'll take it tomorrow," I said. "It takes about an hour." I wanted to do the test at my own apartment. I wanted to be in my own bubble of space and time to process the result. Noah kissed me as he headed out the door. The work crew waited out front in the big white truck; there was no time to talk. "I love ya," he said. The blue box had made Noah a man of few words.

I don't remember much about the test kit. I don't remember the instructions. I only remember the appearance of a small brown ring resembling an ovum. The process was supposed to take about an hour, but it seemed the ring appeared almost instantly. I stared down at it. A strong positive, I'd say. I called Anne immediately. I rarely talked to Mom these days. She was fading away, and Anne had stepped up.

"I need to tell you something," I said, my voice measured. Fear took hold, and with it tears. There was realization in that instant—I was unprepared. "I'm pregnant."

"You're pregnant," she repeated, solidifying the fact.

No doubt about it. Ready or not, I would soon be a mama.

Some decisions you make on faith. You put your trust in another human being, take their hand, and leap. Such was the case with Noah and me. Though we hadn't been dating long, we did care for one another—*love*, I called it at the time, though in hindsight I believe true love takes years to develop. Regardless of our brief courtship, we could see no reason not to stay together to raise our child, though I won't deny we had our share of fears.

"Would you like to marry me?" Noah asked one afternoon after we'd both had time to process the news.

I didn't quite understand the question. It was as though we were at Graham Central Station and he was inviting me to two-step. "Are you asking me?"

"Well, yeah. I'm asking you." he said. "Would you like to marry me?"

The proposal didn't quite fit my ideal, but I'd become

familiar with Noah's cool, logical approach. "Yes," I said. "I'd like to marry you."

It was a warm September evening, the western horizon apricot, the sky a cornflower ombré. The Oklahoma sunset reflected the colors in my bridal bouquet, the colors of good dreams. We were wed in the backyard of Jane and Andrew's home. Noah's family was there, but not all mine could attend. Dad and Mom had recently separated (it had been a long time coming). Mom lived in Milwaukee now, and Katie and Chris lived with Dad in the UP. Everyone was barely scraping by. Janie managed to pay for Mom's trip down. Dad couldn't afford to come. Anne, Katie, and Chris remained home as well. Katie told me later that Dad was sad the whole day. It hurt my heart. "He wanted to walk you down the aisle," she said. I missed everyone, but I knew money was tight.

As the keyboardist played a simple wedding march, Andrew, dressed in a navy suit, stood in for Dad. He was the one to walk me down a sheet of white plastic laid atop freshly mowed Bermuda grass. Andrew and Janie's cat escaped the house and proceeded to make figure eights between my feet, its tabby tail protruding from beneath my gown. I couldn't stop laughing. The pastor didn't know what to make of it. Before Andrew left my side, he lifted my hem slightly, his taut bronze face contorted in amusement, his teeth white as tan lines. He dramatically snatched the cat from the scene like the Grinch, pitapatted back down the aisle with it, and locked it indoors for the duration of the ceremony. More of his humor.

We had a small wedding budget. Noah's oilfield job and my position as a secretary for a construction company provided only moderate income. I'd started working full time shortly after I graduated high school. I had attended one semester at Oscar Rose, but my dreams of attending the University of Oklahoma, or any college for that matter, had taken a back seat to financial survival. Each pay period, Noah and I set a little aside for wedding expenses. His parents purchased his suit and the cake. Andrew and Jane helped with reception expenses, and our two attendants purchased their own dress wear. As for my gown, I managed to find one within budget one Saturday afternoon in late July.

I had driven to north Oklahoma City that day—to the stretch where the money was. I'd seen a sale ad in the newspaper for a bridal boutique in the area. It was a long shot that I could afford anything in the store, but I thought I'd take a peek. A bell chimed as I entered, the sound swiftly doused by plush carpeting and the clouds of white billowing from the racks. Classical music played overhead, a sure sign these goods were out of my reach. But I was there now. I might as well take a look.

There were no other customers in the store that I could see, only a salesclerk busying herself behind the counter. I hadn't yet moved from the door, unsure what one was supposed to do in a store such as this. Could I just *touch* the dresses? Did I need permission? Promptly, the clerk turned her attention to me and approached with a smile. "Good afternoon," she said. Her powdery scent reached me before she did, but it wasn't overwhelming. Her wrists were draped in fine, tinkling bangles, and she wore a crisp, classic skirt and blouse, both rich with texture—the kind you can feel with your eyes. I folded up a bit, feeling gauche in her presence. I had come wearing a blue-and-white romper—one I'd bought at Lerner's—straw flip-flops, and a spritz of Enjoli by Revlon. "How may I help you?" she asked.

She didn't appear judgmental, which eased my discomfort. "I'm looking for a wedding dress," I said. "Maybe something in ivory. For me."

"Of course," she said, nodding. "We have a beautiful selection. Where would you like to start? Do you have any styles in mind?"

"Well…" I paused and glanced around the room. As tempted as I was to try on a flurry of elaborate dresses that were out of my league, I figured there was no sense wasting her time. "I heard you were having a sale," I said. Heat rose in my cheeks.

"Ah, yes. We *were* having a sale." She motioned for me to follow as she turned and headed toward the back of the store. As she glided along, she raised an alabaster index finger, the nail well manicured. "I'm afraid we're running low now," she said over her shoulder, "but I think I have one dress that might fit your needs." On the back wall near the fitting rooms, she flipped through the items on the rack with the melon-colored "reduced" sign posted overhead. "Oh, good. I didn't think we'd sold it yet." She pulled out an ivory gown with a flowing skirt and sheer overlay. It had a blouson bodice, long lacy sleeves, and a high neckline. It was perfect.

"Mmm," I said, barely giving it the once-over before I swept it from her hands and ducked behind the heavy curtain of the fitting room. She offered to assist, but I declined, except for zipping up the back, which try as I might, I couldn't pull off on my own. The gown fit suitably off the rack and was marked eighty dollars, "Last season's." I purchased it on the spot and delivered it immediately to Jane's house, where I stashed it in her closet for the next six weeks.

On the eve of our wedding, I was lucky to get the dress zipped again. My belly had blossomed. I was entering my second trimester when Noah and I said "I do" and kissed, perhaps a little too passionately, in front of an intimate group of family and friends who stood clapping as the sun simmered behind the wax myrtles.

Just like that, we were a family in the making.

GENERATIONS

The contractions began around ten thirty on a Thursday night. I was lying on my side of the sloshy waterbed when the first pain struck. There was a sudden shift in my pelvis, a sharp, forceful cracking in the bones between my hips, like the shell of a lobster giving way after boiling. It scared me. I lay still, waiting for Noah to return home from bowling league. He was my safety now.

It was nearly five months to the day since our wedding, and though I couldn't be sure, I felt our baby might finally be ready for its grand entry. We had no idea if it was a boy or a girl, but we preferred the surprise. We had painted the nursery a unisex mint green and purchased only gender-neutral outfits. I even had a unisex baby name in mind, though somehow, intuitively, I suspected I was carrying a girl. That's what I really wanted—little girl clothes were so cute. We had an ultrasound, but I couldn't make heads or tails of the screen. It was all one grayscale blob to me. I should have listened to my doctor, whose tools of the trade amounted to a cold stethoscope and a cloth tape measure. He was an old-school obstetrician.

"You don't need that to have a baby," he said to me at one visit. "Women have been having babies for eons without all these electronics."

"But I'd like to see it," I said. "I'd really like to have an ultrasound." I hadn't even heard the baby's heartbeat. And I was in my third trimester by this time.

"Fine," he conceded. "You wanna see it, you can set it up down the hall. They do that in their office. But I'll say again, it's just an extra unnecessary expense."

Turned out in this case he was correct.

Now, my bulbous belly and I lay enveloped by the water-bed mattress. Outside, Noah's pickup pulled in beneath the carport. His headlights faded. I heard the warm clop of his worn boot heels upon the pavement and the soothing sound of his key in the lock—the lock to the house we shared with Gram's guitar and a German shepherd named Max. My tension melted.

Noah had a calming way about him. He was steady and honest, rational and pragmatic—all desirable counterweights to my own emotionalism. He was grounded by strong roots, having lived in the same community his entire life. I envied that in him, admired it. He'd gone through one school system, graduating with the same kids he'd grown up with. His parents were a solid, constant pair who had lived in the same home since he was three years old. *Three years old!* I couldn't imagine. He'd purchased a home just a few miles away. They helped him with the down payment, which he repaid in time. I liked that about him too. I liked that he seemed conscious about finances and tried to do the right thing, a fact that became more apparent to me when we went ring shopping one evening before the wedding.

"Remember," he said. "We can only buy what we can afford." We were standing in front of a jewelry display, facets glinting, tempting me.

"Well, what we can afford?" I asked.

"Whatever we can pay cash for." He didn't believe in credit cards.

So that night we purchased two gold bands. His was smooth and mellow in tone, mine bright and delicately etched—a hint more dramatic. "They don't match," Noah said. He was worried about that, but I didn't mind. The rings were complementary. They represented who we were as individuals, and who I hoped we would become as a married couple.

He tiptoed into our tiny bedroom now, arched bowling bag in hand. I lay still and quiet, warmed by the hint of cinnamon in his fading cologne. He hopped a time or two beside the closet trying to peel off his boots, a bit playful from bowling alley beer. He smelled of Saturday nights—of riding in the Silverado, of "Billie Jean" and the Gap Band. I watched him as the weak light of a winter's moon yawned through the miniblinds. "I think I'm in labor," I announced in the dim.

His head snapped in my direction. He must have thought I was asleep. "Are you serious? You're gonna have the baby tonight?"

"I don't know about tonight, but maybe in the morning."

"Are you okay?"

"Mm hmm. I'm okay. The pains are far apart." I'd only felt two contractions, separated by exactly sixty minutes. Instinctively, I knew to time them. Instinctively, I knew what they were.

"Well," he said, one boot on and one boot off. "I wonder if I should even get undressed."

"You can go to bed. I'll wake you if I need you."

"You almost got this, babe," Noah said, coaching me. He looked drained and parched. "You almost got it. Just a little bit more." He slipped an ice chip into the side of my mouth. He could have used one himself.

"Okay, Theresa," the doctor said. "Bear down. Last time now, dear. Nice big push."

It was nearly ten thirty again—almost twenty-four hours later. I was exhausted and in a fog of Demerol, which was the doctor's choice of pain management for back labor. I looked down my trunk, at the V formed by my legs hitched in metal stirrups. Suddenly, the white-haired doctor boosted a blue-tinged bundle of limbs and head. I could see a tiny rump. Legs unfurled, wet and shiny. I saw a thin rope-like organ dangling from between. My head fell back on my pillow; I couldn't hold it up anymore. "It's a boy," I announced, mildly disappointed.

"No," the doctor said. "A nice healthy girl."

"*What?*" My head shot up again. "A girl?"

Noah was laughing. "It's a girl," he exclaimed, and kissed me. I worried about my breath—we *were* newlyweds, after all. "You got your girl!"

The nurse had taken our baby and was suctioning out her mouth and nose, wiping her down and measuring. "What a perfect size," she said. "She's a good weight. Nine pounds four ounces. You won't be afraid to hold her."

"Nine pounds?" Noah repeated, surprised.

"Nine pounds four ounces," the doctor mumbled. "That's a big girl."

"I can't believe it's a girl," I said. "I thought I saw a penis."

"Probably the cord," the doctor said. He was still at work between my knees, waiting for the placenta to deliver.

"What are you gonna call your baby girl?" the nurse asked. "Do you have a name picked out?"

I glanced at Noah in case he had changed his mind about the name, but he was just smiling. "What's her name?" he asked.

I looked back to the nurse. "Her name is Jackie."

PART THREE

ROCK-A-BYE

J ackie was an ash-blonde, curious toddler when the brown Trimline trilled in the hallway of the little brick house on Fifty-Second Street. I crossed to the vintage telephone cubby heaped with phone books and takeout menus. "Hello?"

I was surprised to hear Mom's voice on the other end of the line. Since last I'd seen her some two years ago, she had nearly disappeared, with the exception of birthday cards. She was still in Milwaukee working as a nursing assistant, though I'd heard she was having trouble holding down a job. "Hi, Trese! It's Mom." Historically, those words had often been followed by statements of considerable shock value. I braced myself, and rightly so. After a brief spate of uncomfortable small talk, the announcement arrived. "Guess what," she said. "I'm gonna move back to Del City. We're gonna rent an apartment there." Regardless of her age, Mom had a youthfulness about her, a naïveté. Always had. It was what made her lovable but vulnerable as well. Her childlike excitement snaked up my coiled phone cord. I squeezed the coils where they met the receiver, tried to cut her energy off at the pass. I could only deal with my own emotions at the moment.

"You're moving to Del City?" I asked, mind whirling. Given her current lifestyle, the thought of Mom living nearby tweaked my gut in all the wrong ways. But it was the "we" part that really cinched my innards. The "we" part involved a man Mom had recently taken up with, someone none of us considered to be a healthy influence. No, we didn't hold him responsible for Mom's choices—those were hers—but it didn't take much imagination to see the flaws in his character. We had witnessed her steady decline ever since they'd first met, and though we all hoped the arrangement would run its course quickly, it dragged on like a lame deer.

"Are you surprised?" she asked.

I was most definitely surprised.

"It'll be a week or so before we get down there. I'll call you when we're settled."

Mom and I had a tenuous relationship at best in those days. Looking back, I suppose it had been that way for years, perhaps since the trip to West Virginia. We nested on a weakening branch. But it was in the weeks after my daughter's birth when the bough broke.

Mom had called me one spring day to announce she wanted to come see the baby. "I want to come visit you for a few days," she said. "Help you out a little."

Though our house was small and Noah and I were still adjusting to one another, to the baby herself, the elusive hope of normalcy in my family enticed me to agree. "Okay," I said. "That would be nice." I had just turned twenty-one, and though Noah's mom had tried to offer support to me as a new, nervous mother, sometimes a girl just needs her own mama.

In preparation for her visit, Noah and I cleared the junk in the spare room, which had once served as a single-car garage. We stacked it all neatly to one side, including Janie's belongings—Janie had by this time joined my siblings up north after she and Andrew had unexpectedly parted ways. She had left town quickly and returned home to heal, and Noah and I had stored her things until she could collect them. With the burgundy shag carpeting now visible and vacuumed, we borrowed a mattress from a friend and laid it on the floor. I scraped together some fresh sheets, blankets, and a pillow. Despite its multipurpose status, the room looked neat and tidy, albeit a throwback to the early seventies, and I was relieved Mom would have some privacy. I wanted her to feel welcomed.

"We should really make better use of this space," I said to Noah when we were finished.

"Let's finish the kitchen first," he said.

A few days later, night had fallen and Noah and I were lounging on the sectional his parents had bequeathed to him when they redecorated their home. The television was on and the baby was tucked away in bed. Behind us, there was a gentle tapping at the storm door, which opened directly into the living area. The door popped open before we could rise. Mom's head appeared around the jamb. "Hello," she said. Her smile was sheepish. My hairs stood on edge. I sat up as

Noah went to welcome her. "I have a surprise," she said. She disappeared momentarily, then walked in leading a stranger by the hand. "I brought a friend."

My mouth gaped, heart skittered. The alveoli in my lungs collapsed and I gasped for air, like my childhood goldfish must have done when it was flung from its bowl onto the floor. I had agreed to no *friend*. I had only agreed to her. As she introduced us, the rule-bound part of me demanded I be respectful, but I was wary and aloof. I didn't reach for the stranger's hand. I didn't welcome him. How could I? He *wasn't* welcome. I felt Noah's eyes on me, questioning. As they returned to their car to collect their bags, there was a roar in my ears, a throb in my veins. I could think only three words: *Make him leave! Make him leave! Make him leave!* But that would require courage, and courage took time to conjure. When the stranger reappeared in our living room, he clutched a case of beer in his thin, pale hands. We never kept beer in our house. The twenty-four pop-tops sneered at me as they passed, violated the sanctity of my home. He dashed into our kitchen to stash them away in our fridge. "Can't forget this," he said. A sound escaped his throat. A gurgle? A chuckle?

At that point I knew courage was my only option. It was too late tonight, but tomorrow he had to go.

The next morning, the sun rose on a bitter day. I don't know how I'd even managed to sleep. Mom and the stranger had spent the afternoon out and about, but when they returned, I called her into my bedroom. We sat on the slim edge of the wooden waterbed frame, which Noah had crafted himself. I tried to be respectful. I tried to be diplomatic. But I was bleeding inside. "I didn't know you would bring someone, Mom," I said. "I'm not comfortable having him stay here." The words tripped out, scrambled for posture, sought formation, like little soldiers sent into battle without proper training. I was unaccustomed to speaking my mind.

Mom's face hardened. Her eyes flashed, then darkened. "What do you mean?" she asked. "What's wrong with him?"

"I don't know him. I don't like him bringing all that beer into my home either." Mom didn't speak, so I went on. "And what about Dad?" Perhaps this wasn't my place, but I chose the battle regardless.

"Your dad and I are over," she said. "I'm not going back with your dad, Trese. He knows that."

"But does he know about *this*?" Despite the past, or perhaps because of it, I felt the need to watch out for Dad.

Her chin jutted. "Well, what do you want me to do?" Anger had wrangled her tongue, slurred her speech. I was walking a fine line.

"You can stay with us. You're welcome to stay. But he needs to go to a motel."

She sighed and fidgeted. There must have been words she wanted to say, but she didn't speak them. "Well, I'll go talk to 'im," she finally said, and left the room.

I sat waiting for her return. Relief trickled over me, warmed my limbs, smoothed my prickly parts. The conversation had gone better than I expected. At least we'd remained calm. Maturity had stepped up, established a sense of order. In the living area I heard the creak and *thwop* of the storm door. I heard a bit of commotion beyond the wall. I went on with my wait, thinking Noah must be going in and out. After some time, he appeared at the bedroom door with Jackie in his arms. "Hey, Trese," he said, brow bent, eyes curious. "Did something happen with you and your mom?"

"Why?" I asked.

"They just packed up and left."

The words ripped through me like a hatchet. I reached for the baby as I passed Noah, made my way to the front door. I had to see it for myself, to confirm it. Outside, the car was backing out of the drive. Mom was sitting in the passenger seat. Our eyes met for a brief, familiar instant. As they eased off down the narrow street, I heaved and shuddered. I pressed my daughter to my chest, hugged her tight, wept into her soft filaments of hair, onto the pulse of her fontanel. Noah was soon at my side. He wrapped his arms around me and our child.

"It's okay, babe." he said. "We're still here. You still got us."

Mom's unexpected relocation to Del City had occurred quietly, without my involvement. In the short time she lived there, I saw her only when she was alone and, despite her invitations, couldn't bring myself to visit her apartment. I know it hurt her, and though that was not my intent, it was the result. I was still hurting, still angry. I had no tolerance left for the sickness that consumed her. I had no tolerance for the stranger either. In my mind, my mother was gone.

I'd tried to maintain a healthy distance, but it had been a rough summer. The thought of her drinking—even twenty-five miles away—kept me on edge. Though she never showed up at my house under the influence, she did, on occasion, call me, as well as my sisters, late at night. The conversations never went well, including one in particular.

"You never talk to me," Mom said, crying. "You never talk to your *own* mother."

"I can't talk to you like this, Mom," I said.

"You'd rather see me six feet under! You all would!"

I'd heard this so many times in my twenty-three years that, right or wrong, I was hardened to it. "I'm going to hang up now. Please don't call me at night like this anymore." I laid down the receiver and went back to bed, though sleep would be a long time coming.

The next morning, Mom showed up out front. I caught a glimpse of her crossing the lawn, head down, mission-bound. My first impulse was to lock the storm door. I was afraid she was still drunk, afraid of the scene that might ensue. I pressed my daughter into the arms of Noah, who stood staring, startled. "Take her to the bedroom," I said, breathless, heart pelting.

"Why?" he asked. "What's going on?" He remained at the ready, waiting to intervene. I could have asked him to shield me, to protect me. And he would have. But this was *my* mother. It was my problem. I would never escape my childhood if I couldn't stand up for myself, for my own.

"Just go," I urged. "Don't come out." I was at the door by this time and had reached down to flip the lock, but Mom was quick and popped it open before it engaged. I placed my body as a barricade in the slice of the opening and stood overlooking her small frame planted there on the artificial grass carpet of my porch. Why was I so fearful of such a small being?

"I just wanna talk to you a minute," Mom said.

I could tell she had sobered up. My breathing eased, but my spine was a rod, vertebrae fused in defense. I said nothing. I didn't step aside.

"I'm sorry about last night," she said. "About calling you like that. You know Mama wouldn't do that if I wasn't drinking."

I had no words.

"Anyways, I wanted to let you know we're leaving," she continued. "We're gonna go back to Milwaukee. We're heading out right now. I wanted to tell you goodbye."

I looked over her shoulder and saw the stranger in the driver's seat. I saw bundles in the backseat. I looked back to her, this withered bloom, this shell, always searching for a place, for peace, never finding it. She looked so weak, so frail. So lost in this life she was caught up in. *Who was she?* Where was my mama? Why had she chosen this life over *us*? My throat narrowed, cheeks flamed. There were words I needed

242

to say, a point I needed to make. I knocked about, a racehorse at the starting gate.

Mom reached up and took my shoulders. She tugged my stiff trunk toward her, brushed soft lips to my cheek. I inhaled her morning-after smell, an evaporation of cologne and booze. Last night's binge still meandered through her arteries. It was an odor difficult to disguise. "Love you, honey," she said as she released me, but the sentiment didn't touch the place it was meant for. It didn't touch me at all. I held it at arm's length, unrequited.

"You know," I said hoarsely, my words thick as resin. "You don't have to live like this. You can get help for your drinking." Her gaze fell to my abdomen. She wasn't listening. Or maybe she was. I don't know. She was as closed off to me as I was to her. *We* were the strangers now. "You need treatment, Mom. I hope when you get back you'll get help."

She nodded. "Mm hmm," she hummed. "Mm hmm." A few seconds passed, silent. "We better hit the road," she finally said. "We got a long drive. All the way back to Wisconsin." She smiled, timid, vacant.

"Okay," I said. "Think about it."

I wouldn't see my mother again for several years.

INDIAN STORIES

When I was a young girl, there were nights in the Hubbell house I would lie awake and listen to Mom tell her Indian stories beyond my bedroom door. She mostly only shared them when she was drinking. Perhaps she needed the liquid courage to feel safe venturing into memory, or perhaps it was the only time she felt anyone would listen. She spoke with a beer-thickened tongue and childlike enthusiasm of a powwow princess and of her grandfather. *He was a great man*, she would say. *He was Fisher Negaunee!* Apparently, he was revered—though that wasn't the term she used, it is what I understood her to mean.

I came to know Fisher Negaunee as an icon, a leader. By the time I was six or seven years of age, I'd come to believe my great grandfather was a *chief* of the Chippewa. A chief! No wonder I was a proud Indian girl. I even carried this belief into adulthood, where I broadcast my misconception openly. Once, when I worked as a paraprofessional in a public school, the teacher asked each person in the classroom to share a fact about ourselves. I announced that my great-great-grandfather was an Indian chief. (I even had the genealogy incorrect, as Fisher was my *great*-grandfather.) A few years ago, I finally discovered my error.

"Wasn't Fisher Negaunee a chief?" I asked Anne.

She shook her head. "No, I don't think so. I think he was just...a guy. Maybe a hunter or a trapper?" She shrugged.

"Oh my god," I said, exasperated. "I grew up thinking he was a chief!"

Sometimes, amidst Mom's Indian stories and despite my better judgement, I would emerge from my room needing to relieve myself. Once, as I passed by her where she sat at the kitchen table in midconversation with Dad, empty Old Milwaukee cans multiplying between them, the whites of their eyes muddied with red, I caught her glance and she stopped me. "Trese," she said. "Did you know that? Did you know your mother is a *Chippewa*? A Chippewa Indian?" She leaned toward me, her body invested in the message.

"C'mon now," Dad said. "She needs to hur'yup and get back to bed." He ushered me along with his palm on my tangled mat of hair. He didn't want to get Mom started on her Indian stories. He'd rather talk politics—or perhaps he knew where her tales might lead.

Over the years, Mom's stories quieted, but before they did, they found a place in my heart—much like Gramma's stories—where I tucked them away and carried them throughout life, unsure what I was supposed to do with them or what they had to do with me, exactly. That would all come much later.

RESERVATION ROAD

It was Janie who began the journey, but we all hitched a
ride.

In 1991, Janie was living on the West Coast, where she
worked as an in-home caregiver. Anne had been pressuring
her to move back to the UP. She missed her partner in crime,
her confidante, and wanted her to come home. "I'll move
back home when I can find a job that isn't nursing and support myself," Janie said. And so Anne kept an eye on the job
market.

It was perhaps June when an interesting job advertise-
ment appeared in the *L'Anse Sentinel*. The Keweenaw Bay
Indian Community's drug and alcohol treatment center was
seeking a house manager. The candidate needed a medical
background. Native as well as Tribal preference would be
given. Anne called Janie immediately. "Try for it," she said.
"You never know."

Jane did apply, and after interviewing during a trip
home over the Fourth of July holiday, she was offered the
job. She was perfect for it: a Tribal member, a former nurse,

and a member of the twelve-step community (Janie attended Al-Anon meetings to help her cope with the alcoholism that surrounded her). But she was well suited for the job in ways far beyond those. She had a deep sense of responsibility, a certain fearlessness, a no-nonsense approach. In other words, Janie was fair, but she took no shit from anyone—and withdrawing substance abusers can really dish it out. She wasn't afraid to stand up for herself. Above all, she had a passion for her culture, and for Native concerns in general, though it didn't occur to her at the time how much that would one day affect the lives of us all.

These days, you'll find KBIC's treatment center on a small plot of land outside L'Anse. But when Janie first took the helm as house manager, the facility was located on the third floor of the old red brick orphanage in Assinins, where Mom had stayed as a child. The Tribe held title to the property now, and the Tribal headquarters was also housed there on the lower floors. The orphanage was long defunct, and the diocese had dispensed of the property years ago, offering it to the Tribe for the sum of one dollar. It felt just and right that the Tribe should assume control of the premises. It felt like a reparation of sorts for all the children who had crossed that building's threshold.

"When I first got there," Janie said, "the place needed work." Funding issues had plagued the facility through the years and conditions had deteriorated. "In the first months,

I spent weekdays training and learning the ropes," she said. "And weekends organizing, cleaning, and scrubbing." She cleaned out closets heaped with materials no one wanted, things from as far back as the orphanage days. Meanwhile, the Council granted miracle funds to improve sleeping quarters and redo bathrooms. As those projects were underway, she dug through floor-to-ceiling piles of vintage church goods like plant stands, urns, and marble lecterns until she uncovered what lay beneath: two spacious sun porches with sweeping windows that looked out on magnificent Keweenaw Bay sunrises.

Amid all the cleaning and organizing and remodeling that went on the first year or so, the project nearest and dearest to Janie's heart was the dining hall, located on the first floor. It was the same dining hall where Mom had passed her tearful young brother when they were children. A dining hall that now fed the troubled adult children of past generations. The worn wood floor was buffed until it gleamed (by paid employees this time, not orphaned children), and the original dish cabinet, a massive structure that took some five men to move, was cleaned, polished and repaired. A home-cooked menu was instituted, a salad bar added. Though at one point in history, the space had served as a cold, industrial food hall, it was now filled with warmth.

Warmth was new to the halls of that red brick building. I'd once read that the Assinins orphanage wasn't as bad as others in the region, but by Mom's account, children still suffered there. It was rumored there were ghosts in the basement. "The staff used to tell me it was haunted down there," Janie said. "They said you could hear things. Children giggling. I don't doubt it." I wondered how the children could be giggling, considering their plight, but I liked the thought that they had found joy somewhere.

While all this physical plant improvement was occurring, Janie was undergoing improvement herself. She was learning how to operate a Native treatment center where culture was an important aspect of programming, including access to traditional medicines and ceremonies central to Native health and well-being. Janie, like the rest of us, had grown up without a deep grounding in Native culture, but with the help of the Tribe and her coworkers, she set out to learn. "They would invite me to everything," Janie said. "To all the cultural events. And I loved it."

Janie began sharing the stories she'd heard, passing them on by word of mouth the way it had been done for generations. She also began to gift us differently: a Native blanket, a dreamcatcher, some medicines for smudging. Once, after she'd given me an abalone shell and a bag of sage, I just stood there holding them, uncertain. "What do I do with this?" I asked her. "Teach me." And she did.

Janie became our conduit to the reservation and its lost lessons. What she shared wasn't just about medicines or gifts or history. It covered all aspects of life, all the bits and pieces of culture and tradition. The past began to make more sense—my *family* began to make more sense—and there was empowerment in that. The set of beliefs I had grown up with seemed less random. There was logic to it. There was history.

Most importantly, Janie's work with the Tribe taught us about alcoholism in the Native community. We learned about the impact of residential schooling and intergenerational trauma, both of which might have played a role in my mother's addiction and her mother's before her. We also learned to identify negative stereotypes about Natives and alcoholism, which I myself had believed based on my childhood experience. We discovered that though our Native family was comprised of many people who struggled with alcoholism, that was not true of *all* Native families. As a matter of fact, Native Americans abstain from alcohol at a rate of nearly 60 percent, compared to some 43 percent of whites.[1] Yes, my siblings and I were at risk of becoming alcoholics because of environmental factors—but it wasn't a predetermined destiny. We had a choice. It was this knowledge that had the strongest effect on Janie.

"I was sick and tired of the ambulance showing up at our house," she said one night while we were discussing life with our parents.

---

1 James K. Cunningham, Teshia A. Solomon, Myra L. Muramoto, "Alcohol Use among Native Americans Compared to Whites: Examining the Veracity of the 'Native American Elevated Alcohol Consumption' Belief," *Drug and Alcohol Dependence* 160, (March 2016): 65-75, https://doi.org/10.1016/j.drugalcdep.2015.12.015

"Or the police," Anne said. "You never knew what was gonna happen."

"I'd had enough," Janie said. "I wanted something different. I wanted a different life. And I knew I drank to get drunk. That had to change. I think I was the first one of us to really commit to sobriety."

Janie said she first realized she too was part of the problem when she attended a women's support conference. "I don't know why I went," she said. "It wasn't a Native function. It was just for women in general. And I wanted to go." She drove the three hours south to the facility that hosted the event. Inside, her life transformed. "A woman got up and told *my* story," she said. "She was *me*, basically. She had lived my life. And that's when I knew." Janie remembers that moment like it was yesterday. "I call it my 'spiritual awakening'," she said. "It wasn't about faith. It wasn't about God. I always believed in God. This was about *me*. *My* spirit. It was about seeing myself for what I was. The addictions *I* had, the codependencies. And once I saw that, a huge weight came off of me. I felt so joyful."

I don't recall ever seeing Janie drunk. I don't recall ever seeing a beer in her hand or a bottle at her lips, so I didn't understand how she had categorized herself an alcoholic. I did, however, understand her when she said she *drank to get drunk*. I could relate. I had done that only once, when I was in high school. It was my junior year. Ben and I had tickets to see Journey in concert at the Fairgrounds Arena. We had been a couple until earlier that day; in spite of the split, we still planned to attend the concert together. He was supposed to pick up me and another friend that evening before the show.

That afternoon, I had scored a pint of Southern Comfort—the whiskey of choice for Oklahoma teens—from an adult coworker. The amber booze sloshed about in its slim container, in short, sharp spikes. Despite my parents' dependence—and my promise to Gramma—I didn't worry much about drinking as a teen. If there was alcohol present, I had no qualms about partaking. That said, however, drinking wasn't a common activity in my friend group, so I didn't spend a lot of time in its pursuit.

I had also finagled that day a tablet or two of a pill dubbed the *white cross*, a common amphetamine, from a well-known source and acquaintance at school. Alcohol was one thing, but drugs quite another. I knew nothing about drugs. The hardest drug I'd ever used was the occasional joint shared in a friend group. Using speed was totally out of character, and to this day I don't remember if I did indeed ingest it. I might have; it was around this time that my siblings and I were climbing out windows onto car hoods, and between that and the fresh break-up, I was feeling reckless.

I started swigging straight from the bottle by four o'clock. By the time Ben showed up, I was barely aware we'd even broken up. The whiskey had done its job well. No wonder my parents craved such things. I recall being giddy and carefree as we drove across town to the arena, but when we parked and exited the car, an incredible tide of self-pity and melancholy overcame me. It cemented my feet to a spot just a few steps away from the Olds. I leaned my head on the wall of a pickup bed and cried. I couldn't move. Couldn't think. I was swallowed up in a pit of despair.

Ben was at my side talking to me. "C'mon, Theresa," he said. "We need to get inside and find our seats. What's going on?" I still couldn't speak. "How much did you drink?" he asked. I don't know if he hoisted me into his car or if I walked. I only remember him lowering me sideways into the bucket seat on the driver's side, so that my legs were hanging out the open door. He let go of me and my trunk careened backwards; my head smacked against the gear shift in the center console. "God," he said. "Are you okay?"

After that, I was moved to the backseat, where the whiskey chose to find its sudden, violent exit. "What did you do?" Ben asked, worried. "What'd you get into?" He was angry and scared, so he left our friend at the arena and drove me directly to the home of a family member who lived on that side of town. I remember the car stopping and Ben jumping out, leaving the driver's door open. Footsteps pounded the lawn. Soon a man's face appeared over me, blocking the fading blue sky.

"What'd you do, Theresa?" he asked. "Let's get ya outta there."

"She said she took some pills," Ben said. "And she's been drinking." By this time the sickness had passed, but a cold indigo had taken its place. Guilt. Remorse. I had upset him, I had ruined the Journey concert. I had become my parents.

I was carried into the house across a vast front lawn where an entire neighborhood could see my head dangling over a crooked elbow. Then into the bathroom, where I was set on the floor next to the toilet. The lid had flowers printed in a cluster at the center. "Look at these pretty little flowers," I mumbled, tracing them with my finger.

"What did you take, Theresa?" the kind man asked. He was standing in the doorway. "Can you tell me what you took?"

"She said it was speed," Ben said. He stood beside him.

"How many'd you take?"

I held up my fingers. First one, then two. Then shrugged. Did I even take any? I remember this instant in time, the two of them standing in the doorway of the tidy bathroom, the concern on their faces.

"Are you sure? Is that all?"

They gave me water and let me sit. I was coming around. Eventually, they encouraged Ben to go on to the concert. He had left our friend there. She would need a ride home. They would drive me back to his mother's house, and Ben could pick me up there and bring me home later.

The next morning was a school day. I awoke with my head pounding, throat aching, parched. How would I survive the day? Across the room stood Gram's bureau, dark, disapproving. She would not be happy with me. As I lay in bed, the door swung open. It was Dad. "Hey," he said. "How you feeling?"

Dad never checked on me in the morning. Did he know something? Was I in trouble? "I'm fine," I said, false cheer in my raw words. "Why?"

"Just checking," he said. "You better get up for school now. You'll be late."

This was the one and only time, to my recollection, that I ever chose to drink my troubles away like that: deliberately, with intent.

I was lucky.

It was 1992. Janie was just about to head to bed when the phone rang. Such occurrences weren't uncommon at this time of night; her job required her to be on call and she'd had to make the thirty-mile drive back to the office on more than one occasion. Turned out the treatment center was a lot like our childhood home—you never knew what might happen.

She picked up the receiver. "Hello?"

It wasn't the office calling. It was Mom. We rarely heard from Mom anymore. We often didn't know where she lived, where she worked, *if* she worked. To be truthful, we seldom knew if she were alive or dead. Now, Janie listened to the desperation on the other end of the line. It was obvious Mom was drunk, but she wasn't calling to threaten. She wasn't calling to guilt her. She was calling for help. "I'm gonna end up dead if I stay here…if I keep up this drinking," Mom said. "Will you come get me? Bring me home?"

Janie had learned enough to establish some ground rules. "Yes, I will come and get you," she said. "And take you to treatment."

Mom was in no condition to argue. She agreed to Janie's offer. She would enter treatment.

Fortunately, Janie knew just the place.

MEMORY

It was the mid-nineties, the holiday season. Noah, Jackie, and I had made the long trip from Oklahoma City to the UP to spend Christmas with my family. We were staying with Janie and her new husband Kurt, a Copper Country fellow, born and bred. We spent Christmas Eve at Janie's place opening gifts and enjoying appetizers, but on Christmas Day the entire family was scheduled to be at Mom's for gift opening and dinner.

A couple years earlier, finished with treatment but still on edge, Mom had decided to put down roots in the Copper Country. She purchased an old, coal-dusted, mining-style house south of Houghton—one she'd found listed for sale in the *Copper Nugget*, a local sales paper. "Wanna come take a look at this house I found?" she asked Anne on the phone one afternoon. "I'm thinking about buying it." They drove up a winding, forest-lined hill to the tiny mining community. The homes were tall and square, in varied stages of remodeling, with a few projects stalled, half-finished—not unusual in the area; money was tight. When they reached the address, they climbed the steep dirt drive to the lemon-yellow house, a vintage box with a steeply pitched roof sheltered by tall, arcing pines. Its exterior wasn't too bad, but inside was a different story. "You sure you wanna buy this?" Anne asked. She feared to venture too far inside. The walls were thick with black dust, the floors like an ash pan. But Mom was undeterred—she was no stranger to living quarters in need of cleanup—and she was energized by her ability to secure the small loan. Before long, she held the keys in hand. She scrubbed the place down and gave the old house new life. It was her first home purchase, one she'd managed all on her own (the stranger was finally fading), and she was damn proud of her accomplishment.

I'd been to her place once before. She'd hosted a picnic over the Fourth of July holiday where we chatted casually, though I was guarded. It was as though a cold, gray blade now hovered over us. It threatened me, like a guillotine. I feared that should it be agitated it might slice me clean through, put an end to me. And so I left it undisturbed. Through the years that blade had become my shadow, not to be shaken.

Christmas night we gathered in the small living area of the mining house. It was a narrow rectangle with a high window, a low sofa against one wall and a television on the other. Senior portraits of my siblings and me hung above the couch. In the corner, the tree was dressed in familiar fashion— Mama's tree, the tree of my youth, all tinsel-wrapped and dripping icicles, multicolored bulbs reflecting memories of Santa. Mom stood beside it, eyes sparkling, spirit beaming, dispensing the gifts she'd purchased. Grandkids squealed and giggled, camouflaged in heaps of crumpled wrapping paper. Katie squealed too, happy to be with Mom on Christmas. Stacks of opened gifts towered around us. Bows accumulated in a plastic bag at Mom's side—she would reuse them in the coming years. Some things never change.

"Oh, this one's for you, Trese," Mom said, and handed me a small box with a polypropylene bow. I was standing nearby and began peeling the bow from the top, picking at the taped points of holiday paper. Beneath the paper was a box, and within the box, a small, acrylic piano. "Here," Mom said. She took the piano from my hand, flipped it over, and wound the golden key on its underbelly. The delicate ping of a tune commenced. Instantly I recognized it: "Memory" from *Cats*. She handed it back to me. "When you play it, I hope you'll think of me," she said. It was a short phrase but a complex one, drenched in sorrow, remorse, grief—all wrapped up in ten little words, all pooled in her hopeful eyes.

Up to that moment, I had not known about my own well of tears, the depth of it, or how it shimmered, waiting, so close to my surface. I was unaware of the sorrow I harbored, how I'd come to exist on its fringes, treading a narrow strip of beach, heels digging in. It all revealed itself, right there in front of my family on Christmas night, soaking my cheeks, stealing my breath.

And my shadow began its slow dissolve.

ZEBA

High on a hilltop overlooking the eastern shores of Keweenaw Bay lies the community of Zeba. I've heard it said *zeba* is the settler's take on an indigenous word—*ziibi*, meaning river—a word rooted in the language of my maternal grandparents. Once a fur trading post and former site of a Methodist mission, Zeba is steeped in Native history. Chippewa from across the region converged upon this spot to trade goods, attend camp, and reconnect with remote family members. The mission church still stands today with its wide bell tower and wood-shingled exterior, looking much the same as it must have some 130 years ago.

Zeba always held meaning in our family, though in my younger years I didn't know why. I'd heard Mom speak of Zeba, of relatives there, of time spent there. I came to view Zeba as a cultural time capsule. They spoke "the language," as Mom would say. I learned that in Zeba, they honored traditions, quietly hosted ceremonies. They laid loved ones in a cemetery where spirit houses marked the graves of those who had walked on. This tiny hamlet had managed to honor its community, maintain the thread of culture. Despite all that was stacked against it, Zeba endured.

It was the mid-1940s when Mom's parents took her by the hand and walked with her to a point in downtown L'Anse. Mom remembers very little about it, only that it was early in the day and they planned to meet up with her Aunt Lydia. Lydia would take them by car to Zeba, located just outside of L'Anse.

Mom usually enjoyed time in Zeba. In the summer she would visit, sometimes for weeks. Her paternal grandparents lived there. She recalled sitting at the table, her grandma serving her toast and Kool-Aid. "She never spoke a word of English," Mom said. "Only Indian." She said she once made the mistake of asking a question in English. Her grandma's eyes popped open wide, her head cocked sideways. "I switched over to Indian real quick," Mom said. "I had to speak it with her. I don't think she understood English."

That day, as Mom and her family stood waiting for Aunt Lydia, Mom wasn't so sure about going to Zeba. Earlier that morning, in the privacy of their home, she had asked her ma what they were doing. Her ma could speak English well enough, but on this morning she spoke "the language." *We're going to ceremony*, she might have said, *niimi'idiwin* or perhaps *maawanj'iding*, but Mom had to mentally translate the words into the language of L'Anse, into English. She heard the Indian language less and less these days, but one thing was clear: They were going to powwow. She said her mother's brow puckered. "Shh," she said, waggling a finger near her lips. *Don't talk about it. Don't tell anyone.* Mom doesn't recall the exact words used, but she knew very well their meaning. You only kept secrets when you broke rules.

"That's probably why I blocked it out," Mom said. "I wasn't supposed to remember."

MAAWANJ'IDING

"You should come up for powwow," Janie said. We were talking on the phone one spring day in 2004. "You haven't been to powwow yet, and you live so close."

Noah and I now lived in Minnesota with our college-age daughter Jackie and our preschooler son, Samuel. The two were born sixteen years and eight hundred miles apart. Our daughter took after the Ottens; our son, in some ways, the Bertineaus, though he definitely had his father's strong jawline. We'd moved to Minnesota in 1998. Noah had left the oilfield in the mid-eighties, returned to school, and taken up a career in the immunodiagnostics industry. He loved his job, but the frequent travel was a stress on our homelife. In time, he accepted an in-house position at the company headquarters in the Minneapolis area. I'd never dreamed I would one day leave Oklahoma, but relocating was a way to have Noah home again. Besides that, Minneapolis was much closer to the UP, and I missed my family. It was a perfect fit in many ways. Yet we were sad to leave behind friends and loved ones in the state we called home.

We decided to make the move before Jackie entered high school. We thought it might be easier for her to acclimate to a new school with an incoming class, but it was a struggle nonetheless. She had roots in Oklahoma City. She had friends. She liked her school. She felt a lot like me when I left lower Michigan at thirteen. I understood.

The transition took another turn when, shortly after moving, I became pregnant with Sam—an unexpected surprise for us all. After a series of miscarriages in the mid-nineties, Noah and I had given up on adding to our family. Though this pregnancy was touch and go in the early weeks, with the help of added progesterone, I successfully carried Samuel to full term. He was a beautiful, healthy millennial baby, weighing in a little less than his sister at eight pounds seven ounces. According to Mom, big babies run in the family.

"I don't know anything about powwow," I said to Janie on the phone. "I wouldn't have a clue."

"You don't have to know anything about it. Just go and watch. It would mean a lot to Mom if you came to see her dance."

My UP family had in recent years begun attending summer powwow, most of them as observers. Mom, however, had her regalia now and danced Northern Traditional. Janie, too, danced the same style, but without formal regalia. She wore an unadorned long skirt and top, draped a fringed shawl over her left arm, and carried a dance fan in the opposite hand. Though I'd never seen either of them dance, Mom had sent me photos from past powwows taken by her new husband Wendell, whom she'd married in 1996. Wendell was also, in part, her regalia craftsman. A local seamstress made Mom's dress, but Wendell was enlisted to assist with the finishing touches, particularly the leather work. He and Mom would design the items together, and he would do his best to help recreate her vision. Wendell wasn't Native, but he was artistic and thoughtful and interested in the culture. He'd also been accepted into Mom's reservation community, where they'd built a home in recent years.

Today Mom's powwow wardrobe includes several dresses from which to choose, but in the early years, she had only one: a crisp, white cotton T-dress with red woven-ribbon trim. In the photos, she stood in a grove of towering red pines. She was flanked by family, a hand-painted shawl draped over her forearm (courtesy of Janie), her black hairline underscored by a red-and-white headband—a gift she'd received in treatment, a reminder of her journey.

It had been nearly a decade now since Mom finished treatment. She'd required two rounds. I still struggled to trust that she was safe, that any of us were. I waited for the other shoe to drop, for the wind to change, for a phone call from one of my sisters telling me Mom had relapsed. That's how we lived our lives—how we'd lived them since childhood, in a perpetual state of negative expectation. Happiness was fleeting. Security short-lived. No good state of being was ever sustainable. It wasn't that we *wanted* bad things to happen. My god. Not at all. We simply knew they would.

And so I waited.

Parked vehicles lined both sides of the highway. Still more cars waited to gain entrance to the Ojibwa Campground, which held the KBIC powwow grounds.

"Wow," I said to Sam, who was buckled into his booster seat in the back. We had driven up from Minneapolis the day before. "Wonder if there's any parking left." We exited the highway and inched along a narrow strip of blacktop in a wooded area. I had driven past the campground's entrance hundreds of times, but I'd never once ventured inside. I had no idea what lay down the road where the cars were headed. Despite the traffic jam, there was a tranquility about the space, a quietude. The trees tamped down the anxiety, the rush, the fear of the unknown. "Pretty here," I said, and reached overhead to open the sunroof. I craved the dapples of sunlight on my skin. I craved the medicine of the canopy.

In the stop and go, I felt the sound before I heard it: bulbous sticks striking stretched hide, the resonance of bass gathering within a wooden frame—perhaps cedar or maple—and escaping in waves. A heartbeat—rhythmic, powerful, life-giving—it pulled at me, drew me in, floated amidst the woods like a spirit. "Hear the drum?" I asked my son. "I feel it in my chest."

He was looking from side to side. "Where is it?" he asked.

"Somewhere off in the trees. We'll see it soon."

We parked some distance away in a grassy area lined with tents and travel trailers, situated between a still lagoon and the waters of Keweenaw Bay. We waited with a burgeoning group of other powwow-goers, each weighed down with folding chairs and cameras, most of them light-skinned. I wondered if they were the tourist crowd. I wondered, too, what I was—what Sam was.

In time, we climbed aboard an aging white van that shuttled us to the cultural center, where we filed out and scattered in all directions. "Let's go find Gramma and Wendell," I said, taking Sam's hand. We strolled along a vendors' row lined with open tents and canopies. The pickle buckets and plastic baskets called to my son, their merchandise irresistible: toy bows and arrows, tomahawks, flutes and hand drums, feathered items of every description. For him, it must have seemed like Disney's Frontierland. He scurried from one tent to the next. *Mom, can I buy this? Mom, can I buy that?*

The drum grew louder; raw, impassioned voices rose in song. Dancers filed past me, cones tinkling with each stride, feathers wafting, footsteps silent, feet swathed in beaded deer hide. They looked to be in a hurry, all focused on the same destination. "What time is it?" I heard dancers asking. One was young, a girl really, frayed braids sweeping an undeveloped breast, wiry frame draped in an ornate shawl, all neon pink and yellow and green. She ran ahead.

Sam and I trailed along behind the dancers. We trailed them past racks of beaded medallions, tables lined with herbs and abalone shells, lassoes of sweetgrass, stacks of fleece blankets, and T-shirts proclaiming *Native Pride.* We trailed them into another culture, into the steam of hot grease, through the thick goodness of fry-bread smell, past signs claiming *Voted Best Indian Taco, Best Fry Bread, Fry Bread Champion.* We trailed the dancers until they disappeared into the smudge of white sage, into an organized logjam, a crush of dancers of every shape and size. So many Native men, auras jingling, roaches nodding, bustles splaying from their lower backs. Like golden pheasants, proud and majestic, they waited at the sloped entrance to the powwow ring. Behind them, women formed in groups: senior leathers, cloth traditional, jingle dancers, fancy shawl. They all looked royal, serene. My chest fluttered and swelled. Somewhere amid that sea of regalia was my mother.

Soon the throng of dancers funneled into the ring, two by two. Sam and I watched from our perch on a hillside where Wendell had set up a line of lawn chairs. We stood beside him, our knees bouncing in rhythm, as at last we caught sight of Mom.

"There she is," Wendell said, beaming. "I wondered what was takin' so long." He looked down at Sam. "See your Gramma there?" he asked.

She looked so small, so lithe, like a sprite. Her skin glowed in the warm July sun and her black hair shone, a single, petite eagle feather pinned snug at the crown of her head. She rounded the curve, eyes down, focused on her step, on the earth, on prayer.

Perhaps she had at last found her place of peace.

GODPARENTS AND GUARDIAN ANGELS

I come from a long line of troubled mothers. I wish I could say definitively that prayer was the answer to ending that cycle. Or powwow. Or Mass. Or pure, simple will. No doubt any of those can serve as a starting point. But in my experience, it took something more to change the trajectory. It took a pair of role models.

As a mother, I made mistakes with my children. Mom made mistakes with me, and her mother with her. Growing up, I heard whispers about Gramma's mistakes too—about her shortcomings as a mother. Though the adults spoke in hushed tones and cryptic language, I knew what they were talking about. I knew Gram's drinking had impacted her children.

Aunty Jean would never say anything negative about Gram in our presence. Instead, she'd laugh about her mother's antics and shake her head. *Your Gramma was a doozy,* she'd say. Aunty Jean was our father's big sister—a bright, sweet, fun-loving woman with glossy apple cheeks and big blue eyes that conveyed a warm humor. She moved away when we were young, but we saw her each year when she came home for the Fourth of July. As children, she was our symbol of Independence Day. The Fourth wasn't complete without her.

When my father died, Aunty Jean became our family's matriarch. She was our guardian angel, watching over us, sheltering us at times. When things got rough, she'd do whatever she could to lift us up, both she and her husband Dan. Throughout the years, Uncle Dan and Aunty Jean never let us wander too far without checking in. No matter where we lived around the country, they found a way to visit. They came to West Virginia twice, Texas once, and Oklahoma as well. It was a comforting custom. I knew we'd never fall completely through the cracks as long as they were keeping an eye on us.

As a child, I was in awe of my aunt and uncle. Aunty Jean was classic and independent and full of moxie. Uncle Dan reminded me of a midcentury television dad—maybe Ward Cleaver or Steve Douglas. Growing up, he was the only person I knew who had attended college, having graduated from Michigan Tech as a civil engineer. To us, he seemed a pioneer.

Once, when they visited us in Texas in 1976, they took me with them on a day-long excursion across the border to Matamoros. They had three children between them, one of whom was grown and on his own by this time, but the other two came with us. The whole family was an adventurous crew. That day, they gave each of us kids a bit of money to purchase souvenirs in the market. "Don't forget your Mexican jumping beans," Aunty Jean said, giggling. She thought no one should leave Mexico without them.

At one stall I followed her advice and bought a trio of the beans in a clear plastic cube. Further down the lane, however, I encountered buyer's remorse when I spotted a rainbow-colored sombrero as wide as a merry-go-round. I was admiring it when Uncle Dan walked up. "Do you have enough money to buy that?" he asked.

"No," I said. "I spent some on jumping beans." I told him what I had left in my pocket.

He looked at the price tag on the sombrero. "*Humph.* You don't have to pay that. You have to barter. Come with me." He took the hat to the vendor and before long I handed over my remaining cash. I walked off down the lane hugging a straw hat nearly the size of my little brother, my grin as wide as its brim.

I'd always felt my uncle loved us girls, but he didn't appear to care too much for Gramma and wasn't as discreet as my aunt with his opinions. One afternoon, shortly after I'd graduated high school, we were all talking about Gram. The subject of beer came up, which set Uncle Dan off. "Your Gramma sure liked *her* beer," he said. "She could have done with a little less of that and a little more—"

Aunty Jean shot him a look. "Dan, Theresa doesn't want to hear that." She was always protective of me when it came to Gramma.

"Well, that's how it was. I'm not saying anything we all don't know."

"I think she can figure things out for herself."

I was too shy to say anything; we all respected our aunt and uncle. They were godparents to most of us girls and, as practicing Catholics, took that role seriously. They did many kind and generous things for us throughout the years, but the most meaningful for me occurred when I was ten years old. It was the week of Gramma's funeral, and Aunty Jean had traveled home from Illinois and was staying with the Haikkinens. All the women were cleaning out Gram's house. I was not invited.

Visiting Lisa one afternoon, heading for the front door, I passed Aunty Jean's train case, which lay open on the floor. It was red with a rectangular mirror lodged in the lid, a gathered fabric lining, and a tray in which you could organize smaller items. It smelled of her, fresh and feminine. In one of the compartments, something caught my eye. It was Gramma's Christmas brooch. I inhaled a loud, wounded breath and stopped dead in my tracks. I looked up at the adults in the kitchen. They'd all been talking—a coffee klatch—cups cradled by spotty digits, but they stood silent now, staring at me. "That's Gramma's," I said, fierce and protective, completely out of character. "I gave that to her for Christmas."

Aunty Jean approached. She laid her hand on my shoulder, feather-light and warm as wings. She reached down to pick up the brooch. "Are you talking about this?" she asked.

I nodded. "Would you like it?" She extended it toward me. "Here. You can have it, Theresa."

I hesitated. We kids knew not to ask for much, but desire got the better of me and I held out my hand. She laid the brooch in my palm. It felt wrong to accept it—most likely, it was one of the few items she had kept by which to remember her mother; Gramma had possessed so little—but I took it nonetheless.

PHOENIX RISING

It was Anne who had the idea.

I received a call from her one late winter afternoon in 2005. "What do you think about making a trip out west to visit Aunty Jean?" she said. "We could surprise her!" Anne loved surprises.

Aunty Jean and Uncle Dan had moved to Phoenix, Arizona, in the early eighties. Uncle Dan had accepted a job out there, but he was retired now. Aunty Jean was suffering with Parkinson's. Though she had done her best to maintain her independence, the disease was progressing, and she'd begun falling more in recent months. Her care became too much for our uncle to handle on his own. They made the difficult decision to move her to a nursing facility.

"Hmm." I stalled for time. "Are we all going?" I didn't want to disappoint her, but the prospect of travel made me anxious.

"Well, Jane and Katie can't go," she said. "But Mom said she'd come. Aunty would be so happy if we all showed up.

Wouldn't that cheer her up?" Her voice bubbled with anticipation and hope.

"Yeah, that would be nice. But you know how I am about flying."

I'd struggled with panic disorder for years, and air travel was a leading trigger. My anxiety was the remnant of a major depression that had struck in my mid-twenties, shortly after my estrangement from Mom. My childhood had finally caught up to me, brought me to my knees. Through therapy I learned I was an "adult child of alcoholics," a phrase I'd never heard before. I learned about the impact of growing up in an environment of addiction and violence and of the effects it still had on me as an adult.

Yes, I would always bear the scars of my exposure to the disease, but I was grateful I had not succumbed to it myself—a gift I never took for granted. I wanted to break the cycle. I wanted the world to be a better place for my kids—and I felt immense pressure to get it right. It took years to overcome the depression; the anxiety hung on. I usually avoided situations in which I'd experienced feelings of panic in the past, a common behavior in panic disorder. Airports were at the top of my list. It took some doing to get me on a plane, and I'd backed out of more than one flight.

"You can do it," Anne said. "Mom and I'll be there with you." (She was trying to be helpful, but it was no secret—Mom was more nervous about traveling than I.)

Despite my concerns, I knew how important the trip was and how much it would mean to our aunt. It was a small recompense for all she had done for us. "Okay," I said. "I'll try."

"Yay!" Anne said. "Aunty'll be so happy." She had no idea what my commitment entailed.

As expected, in the weeks leading up to the flight, my anxiety snowballed. If I thought about the trip, I had palpitations and shortness of breath. I was jittery, obsessing about plane crashes and fretting about leaving my kids. As the trip drew near, I considered canceling, but deep down I didn't want to give in. I didn't want "it" to win. I clung to the thought of bringing Aunty Jean some cheer.

"How're you feeling about your trip?" Noah asked one day. He must have sensed my distress. He knew this would be a challenge for me—he'd guided my sedated self through many an airport and held my hand during take-offs.

"Don't ask," I said. "I don't wanna think about it."

"Trese, you'll be okay. You always do just fine."

"Let's not talk about it now." Avoidance was a coping skill I had mastered.

My anxiety was crippling, but one night I found respite from it—not through medication, as I sometimes did, but through a familiar dream. It had been years since Gram had visited my dreams. As an adult, I was doing okay. I lived a fairly stable life aligned in predictable patterns. In contrast to my youth, my husband and I both had steady jobs. Our children were healthy. The bills were paid. Our home was peaceful. I think Gram knew that I was doing all right now and didn't need her the same way I did in my youth. My spirit dreams had faded.

It was just days before the trip to Phoenix when that changed. Sleep had been fitful for weeks, but one night it ribboned in like a seiche, sweeping me off into the depths where dreams tread and spirits drift. I found myself in the front yard of the Mason house, not the driveway as I had in dreams past. It was a glorious UP summer day. Beside the highway, the leaves of the sugar maple sifted the sun. Rays drenched my blouse and warmed my back. Tendrils of breeze caressed my skin while from the canopy warblers tweedled as if to say, *Welcome, Theresa! Welcome home!* I climbed the steps of the old front porch, the one that led to the abandoned doorway, and stood on the landing steeped in the pungent breath of moss. When I was a child, Gramma wouldn't allow me to play on the porch. She worried it wasn't sturdy enough, feared it would collapse beneath me. But now I stood there like I belonged.

On either side of the door were the windows I had looked out so many times: the one overlooking the record player in the front room and the one to Great-Grampa's old bedroom, where Gram and I had slept in her last days as headlights washed the aqua walls. I waited, knowing, and soon she appeared, her face achingly familiar, drawing me to the bedroom window. Overcome, I leaned from the porch, stretching to get as close to her as I could. I drew so close I saw my own reflection in the pane. I saw that I was no longer a mixed-up girl but a woman—an Indian woman—cheeks striped with tears, pain flooding my eyes. Clearly I had aged, but *her* features endured—the pale cameo of her lips, sienna flecks in her eyes, oil in her hair, lines in her skin. It was the first time her visage had come to me so vividly in many, many years. So many, in fact, that I feared I had forgotten what she'd looked like. I had never come this close to her in past dreams. I had mostly been afraid to set foot on the porch lest her image vanish—but here I was, nearly face to face with her.

I pressed my palm to the fragile glass. "Gramma," I wept. "I'm scared." I went straight to the heart of it— divulged my demon. Perhaps I knew how brief her visit would be.

In past dreams I had spoken but she had not. On this night, that changed as well. "It'll be all right," she said. Her lips were still, but I heard her voice, the words concise and simple, consistent with my own. She too held her palm to the glass—the unyielding transparence between life and death, flesh and spirit—and pressed it opposite mine. "Everything'll be all right."

Her voice filled me with light and elation, bittersweet though it was. It healed me, cauterized my wounds. I didn't want to let go—didn't want her to leave me. I held on as long as I could, palm to palm, soaking her in. Soon, though, her image faded, replaced by the reflection of the maple at my back, the familiar glints of sunlight winking among its branches.

And then she was gone.

The next morning I awoke immersed in a familiar aura. There was a renewed sense of peace and assurance. A calm. I stared at the popcorn-textured ceiling, relieved. Thank you, Gram. Thank you. I knew she had come to tell me it was safe to fly—she *wanted* me to take this trip. I knew the visit was her way of taking care of both her daughter *and* her granddaughter. Sometimes, one simply knows.

My mission clear, off to Phoenix I flew.

Uncle Dan met us at the airport. He offered each a weak, warm embrace. He'd been a tall man but seemed smaller now, his shoulders wilted, his blue eyes dulled. Caring for his wife had drained him. Beneath an atypically gray Phoenix sky, we loaded our bags in the trunk of his car and drove along flat streets past withered palms until we reached the townhome he had shared with his wife. Inside, as I recall, there were few windows to let in the light, and it was still and quiet. It was as gray in there as it was outside. I missed the pop of energy their previous homes had possessed—Aunty's energy. We settled in for the night.

"What time would you guys like to head over to see Jean?" he asked as he retired for the evening.

"How about just before lunch?" Anne suggested. "I brought a surprise for her, and Mom's got something planned too." She seemed inordinately cheerful, as though she felt the void too and needed to fill it.

"Lunch would be a good time," he said. "She's usually alert then."

The next morning, I came downstairs to find Mom and Anne busy in the kitchen. Mom was dicing vegetables. "Whatcha makin', Ma?" I asked.

"I'm gonna make a few pasties," she said. "I wanna take one up to Jean. I'll leave some here in the freezer for Dan too." Pasties were a Cornish miners' dish—a meat pie of sorts—and a staple for most people in the UP, regardless of ethnicity. Gramma often made pasties for us as children and, to this day, we make pasties too. Even the seniors at the Tribe make pasties and sell them as a fundraiser.

"Ooh, I bet Aunty hasn't had a pasty in a long time. She'll love that." Anne was busy at the stove. I could smell something cooking, peeked over her shoulder. "What are you up to?" I asked. The two of them were like a sisterhood, working together for a common cause. Had Janie come along, she would have been right in there with them. It was like that a lot with Mom and my two older sisters. They knew how to tend a village. As one of the younger kids, somehow I'd missed out on that lesson.

"I'm trying to cook up a couple hot dogs," she said. "Vollwerth's." Her brows bounced. She had brought with her from Hancock a package of Vollwerth's wieners, a local brand we'd all grown up with, including Aunty. You couldn't beat the taste of a Vollwerth's hot dog roasted over hot coals. The flavor zapped you straight back to childhood. Anne didn't have a grill, but she was cooking it the best she could to get a similar result.

As planned, we arrived at the nursing home just before lunch and trailed Uncle down a long, germicide-scented hall lined with stainless-steel grab bars. He entered a door about midway down. Aunty was lying on the bed, eyes closed, mouth open. "Jean," he said. "You have some visitors."

My aunt's eyes popped open. She looked at him, blank. No words.

Mom was the first to approach. She padded over lightly, stood inches away, leaned in. "Hi, Jean." She spoke delicately, sweetly, as if greeting a baby bird.

Aunty's eyes lit up. An expression formed. She worked to manipulate her facial muscles, to emerge from beneath the mask of Parkinson's. "Oh! Oh!" She tried to raise her head off the pillow. "Peg?" She had always called Mom by that name.

"It's me," Mom said. "We came to see you." She took her hand and gave it a gentle squeeze and hugged her around the neck, kissing her cheek.

Aunty stumbled over her words. "I opened my eyes and thought I was seeing things." She giggled in her warm, familiar way. I thought of the Mexican jumping beans.

Anne, a nurse who had worked in elder care for years, situated Aunty on the mattress. We all greeted her, but Aunty still didn't trust her eyes. She kept repeating how she couldn't believe it. Uncle Dan suggested we put her in her chair and bring her out to the sitting area where it was brighter and we could talk. She needed to empty her bladder first, so Anne and I wheeled her into the tiled restroom. I had no idea how to transfer her to the stool, but Anne did. The only thing I needed to do was pull the chair out of the way and help with her clothing. As Anne supported our aunt's body against the length of her own, the two started giggling.

"We're dancing," Aunty said. She was becoming more like herself with each passing moment.

Anne laughed. I was surprised when she began to sing an old Judy Garland tune. She must have been listening to Gram all those years too.

> *Put your arms around me, honey, hold me tight,*
> *Huddle up and cuddle up with all your might.*

Aunty Jean gleefully pitched in a word here and there. In her youth, she had sung along with Aunty Lil in the clubs in the UP, wearing a fancy cowgirl outfit. She had also traveled the states with a country-and-western band, singing and yodeling. She was definitely an Otten.

I watched the two of them, thankful for all that had transpired to get me there. Afterward, we all circled up in the lobby. Uncle Dan said he would run some errands and be back to pick us up later. We four women talked for some time while Anne fed our aunt bits of hot dog from a foil pouch. Watching Aunty Jean, I realized how much she had begun to resemble Gramma. I had never thought that before. Aunty Patsy had always *looked* the most like an Otten. But now Aunty Jean's hair lay straight, her bangs fractioning her forehead. In youth her hair color had been blonde, but it was ashy now, as Gramma's had been.

When she finished her hot dog, I pulled my chair up closer. "Aunty," I said, "I need to tell you something." She turned toward me slowly; movement cost more now. I began to tell her about Anne's call and how much I wanted to come, but how difficult it was for me to fly these days. I told her I'd thought I might have to back out, but something happened to change that. "Gramma came to me in a dream," I said. A well of heat swelled in my chest. It rosied my neck and face. Was it ludicrous to believe in dreams this way? I lacked a sense of community around my patchwork of beliefs. I lived far from family, far from Baraga County, far from others who believed as I did. Did Aunty think me nuts?

I pressed on, compelled to share this with her—to let her know what the dream meant. "She told me I'd be safe if I came. She *wanted* me to come see you." Aunty said nothing, only gazed at me, her expression submerged so deep within her eyes I couldn't reach it. Unblinking. Unreadable. Did she understand? Was she offended? I knew their history, but I needed to fulfill this duty entrusted to me. I needed to make sure she understood. "She was trying to take care of you, Aunty."

A hint of acknowledgement broke in her eyes. Soft. Sad.

PROMISE BRIDGE

I only go home once or twice a year now. The seven-hour drive is a challenge for my joints due to arthritis, a condition I share with my siblings. I'll pack my citified SUV with outerwear for all seasons (you never know what weather in the UP will bring), fill my tank at the local Kwik Trip, and head east. I'll tool through the outskirts of Minneapolis, across South St. Paul, and traverse the vast, sparkling St. Croix into Wisconsin before heading north through the woods, where concrete gives way to conifers.

Once, when my son was young, he fell asleep in central Wisconsin on our way to Mom's house, where we stay now—her sobriety a state I've come to rely on, though with watchful eyes. Sam wasn't usually much of a sleeper on car rides. He preferred to stay awake, sharing LEGO stories with his captive audience. I enjoyed his company, but the silence of an occasional nap was always welcome, like a rest stop on an empty stretch of highway. My daughter was in college at the time, so it was just the two of us on this trip. He awoke a couple hours later as we entered the UP. "Are we in the Endless Woods now?" he asked.

"Yep. Only a couple more hours to Gramma's," I said, smiling at him in the rearview mirror. After that day, the stretch between Land O'Lakes and Mom's place was forever known as "the Endless Woods." That was how my son measured how long it would be before we reached *his* gramma's house, where pasties and Jell-O cake awaited. Mom had become to him, in some respects, what Gramma had been to me.

I'm the only one of us to have left the nest of the Keweenaw and not yet returned. Mom and Wendell still live on the reservation, both active with the Tribal seniors, Mom always working to better herself. She's a college graduate now—a lifelong dream achieved with the help of the Keweenaw Bay Ojibwa Community College. This was no small feat considering her education had always been hampered by alcohol: first as a child affected by her parents' alcoholism, and then as an adult foiled by her own. For a shy Indian girl from the sticks, that red cap and gown stood for far more than just a diploma.

Further down the road a ways from Mom and Wendell's place live Janie and Kurt. Janie is retired now, but she'll always be a champion of sobriety. And for our family, she'll always be a cultural leader too. It's natural for her. She follows that drum. I hear the beat too, but I'm still a bit of a wallflower. I feel I've only begun to learn just how much there is to being Native.

Once, while we were living in West Virginia, my fifth-grade class studied dictionary skills. We were to look up a word and write down what we learned. I chose to look up the word "Chippewa." I flipped through the Cs until I found it: "Chippewa," it read. "Term for Ojibwe. A name given by the English to a large tribe of North American Indians." Ojibwe? I'd never heard that before. Why'd they change our name? When my teacher called on me to recite what I learned, I told him my word choice and what it meant.

"And why'd you choose that word, Theresa?" he asked.

"Because *I'm* a Chippewa." It was the first time I'd ever spoken of my Indian heritage to classmates, or in public at all as I recall—not out of fear or shame; it was simply never required of me at that age. The kids turned and stared. I didn't blush a bit despite my inner glow—just like the one that welled up when Gram and I rode through Chassell.

My teacher smiled and nodded. "That's very interesting," he said. "Good word choice." He went on with the lesson, diffusing the stares. He was one of my favorite teachers. I had a lot of good days in that classroom. They helped make up for a lot of bad nights at home.

Having grown up under mostly settler influences, as adults, my siblings and I now embrace our Native heritage—a right denied to my grandparents and to my mother when she was young. Use of the term "Chippewa" has faded in our Tribe, replaced by the decolonized term *Ojibwe*. We've learned that as Ojibwe we are part of a greater collective, the Anishinaabeg—large communities of Native peoples surrounding the Great Lakes in the U.S. and Canada. These communities share similar language and culture. I've come to learn of their history and their struggles, those of all indigenous peoples of North America. I've come to know the story of how another man's culture—one which makes up a quarter of my own blood—devoured that of the Anishinaabeg and bleached the landscape, eroding their spirit. Mom's family had long mourned this devastating loss, as had most on the reservation. Like Mom herself, perhaps my grandparents expressed such pain through addiction. Though their home eventually faltered along that path, Mom always cradled remnants of the ideal: her first glimpse of a newborn brother, gratitude for an uncle's guidance, memories of a parent's humor. She called her father "Papa," a white man's word, not "*Noos,*" as she may have called him in Ojibwemowin—the language of the Ojibwe—which was what my grandparents often spoke in their home. *Oh, my girl,* her father would say to her endearingly, foreign syllables uttered with Anishinaabe meter. My grandfather's language was not the last of his liberties to be stripped away, though it may have been the most painful.

Having left so many years ago, Mom is now rediscovering the traditions our tribe works to restore—those which were lost to her long ago. We have honored her as an elder, danced beside her at powwow, and shared feasts in celebration. We've cleansed our homes with the four medicines, sheltered within protective boughs of cedar, offered *asemaa* in respect, and some, with the help of Jane, have earned treasured eagle feathers. Most importantly, we've learned being Native is not only about ceremony but about mission, about standing for ancestral history, hallowing both the past and present sufferings of our people while working to heal wounds and build our future. That, in my eyes, is what "tribe" is all about.

Mom has even shed her fear of dreams and visions, thanks to the assurance of a traditional healer, a *nenaandawi'iwed*, who was able to put her at ease after a particularly troubling episode. She shared his teaching with me recently after I mentioned an experience I'd had while staying with her one summer years ago. I remember it happened during the month of July. My son and I were visiting—our first visit since his birth.

It was a warm night. The windows were open, but the air was still. I awoke in the dark and checked on my son in the next room. It was cooler in there, so I sat down on the floor beside the window and rested my forearms on the sill. Outside I could hear the carol of the crickets. I could see the wash of a white moon above the stand of woods behind the house. I was absorbed in the moment—the beauty of the scenery, the wonders of a Keweenaw night so familiar to me from childhood. I noticed something then amidst the trees, flashing movement, glints of light. At first I thought it was fireflies, but soon their breasts began to bloat, their luminescence to expand. I watched as they ballooned, drifting higher and higher up the trunks, sliding up the bark until they were suspended in the treetops. By then the glowing orbs were as big as beach balls. I rubbed my eyes and turned away, not trusting what I saw, but when I looked back, there they were: dozens of them, hovering beneath the heavens. Suddenly, from somewhere deep within the woods came the shriek of a bird, perhaps an owl, jolting me. It rang out twice, penetrating the bush. Fear overtook me, and I sank down upon the carpet. I crawled over to my son's side and, despite the heat, pulled an afghan around me. They must be lightning bugs, I told myself. But the gnawing inside said otherwise.

The next afternoon, I told Jane about the experience. I told her how frightened I had been, but she didn't look the least bit concerned. "The spirits can appear that way," she said. "They can take any form." She felt certain I'd had a vision of our grandfathers and grandmothers, but I questioned the validity of this explanation. Up to then, spirits had only visited me through dreams.

When I mentioned this same experience to Mom years later, she had no doubt either. She told me what the traditional healer had taught her. "They come to visit," she said. "To help you."

"But it's scary." Some Indian ways frightened me. I'd been raised with so little understanding.

"That's your Negaunegezhick blood," she explained. Negaunegezhick was the full name of my great-grandfather before it was shortened through assimilation. "That's your Indian. Don't be scared o' that."

I'm still working on it.

Though Mom was able to find healing, Dad's struggles with alcohol persisted. He passed away several years ago, having lived out his days in the Hubbell house. He remained fond of Mom, probably loved her, throughout his life, and never remarried. After the divorce, us kids stayed in touch with him, and our children knew him as Grampa. I came to accept there had been two male parent figures in my life: Jack was my father, but Derry was my dad. I think even Anne came to feel that way. By her early twenties, she was calling him Dad too. The two of them grew closer through the years, and she tended to him as one of her own until he drew his last breath.

Like Janie and Mom, Anne still lives in the UP. There she dotes on her growing flock of grandkids. Katie lives a couple miles from her, across the Portage from my brother and his family. When you're born in the Copper Country, it can be tough to leave it behind.

Whenever I go to visit, I'll make my rounds through life's landmarks. I'll head east out of Hancock and follow the old railroad route along M-26. The tracks are gone now, replaced by a wide-open trail popular with snowmobiles and ATVs. This trail is my guide. It meanders along the Portage for a bit, past the remaining sandstone Quincy buildings that once populated the shoreline, through the little town of Ripley, then into Dollar Bay, where I lose sight of the Portage. I'll pass the place on the corner where Aunty Lil used to sing—it was Sis's Club back then, but it's called Quincy's now. The highway winds through a divide of aspen and birch, with homes dotting the ridge to the north, and in the distance I'll see a green sign with white block letters: "Mason." I'm never truly home until I've seen that.

The town of Mason, along with whatever mining ruins remain there, is now listed on the National Register of Historic Places. The old reclamation plant was demolished in the early eighties—Gram's timber wolf at last displaced. But not too much has changed beyond that. Johnson's old car lot, now full of rusted vintage trucks, remains the gateway to town after all these years. I'll slow to a crawl as I reach the familiar saltbox sandwiched between the pavement and the snowmobile trail. The tightness in my chest reminds me that I still grieve its loss. The white clapboard siding of the house is gone now, hidden beneath brown vinyl. The tree cover has thinned, but there is still ample shade. The porch steps have been demolished and the shed swallowed up by a small addition jutting out to the west. The outhouse is long gone. Before the home was altered too much, my brother-in-law lived in it for awhile, long before he met my sister.

"Guess where Kurt used to live," Jane said to me once, not waiting for an answer. "He lived in Mason—in Gramma's house. He rented it."

"*You did?*"

"It had a bathroom," she said. "Tell her about it, Kurt."

Kurt leaned back in his recliner. "Yah, upstairs. At the back of the house."

"Where the attic used to be," she added. "Where'd you sleep, honey?"

"Um…" He thought for a moment, trying to picture it in his head. "The room off the kitchen."

"The parlor," Jane said, nodding her head. "He didn't like living there."

I bristled at the thought of anyone not liking Gramma's house.

Quincy eventually gave up all its Mason properties and offered them for sale to their tenants. My cousin's family purchased their home, the one where Great-Grampa Otten had originally lived. Lisa still owns it to this day. I've joked with her on occasion about buying my own Mason house, and she's laughed about playing Barbies again. I wouldn't mind living in Mason, I don't think—especially if it were in Gramma's house—though I've heard it continues to change with time. One's home is one's home, and that was mine. If there's anything I've learned over the years, it's that we don't always get to choose where our roots are.

Beyond Gram's house there's still the same vacant lot, then her neighbor's abandoned T-shaped house, a skeleton now, emaciated. A little further down the highway, my cousin's place is well kept and remodeled. Across the road, Aunty Lil's house with the gingerbread kitchen has been sold and resold. Uncle Cecil's house is occupied by another family now. Its golden shutters have gone sandy.

The stretch of highway beyond Mason hugs the shoreline of Torch Lake, which in 1986 was named a priority Superfund by the Environmental Protection Agency. Much cleanup has been accomplished in the area, but it's not yet completely free of hazards. The National Park Service moved into the Copper Country in the mid-nineties and created the Keweenaw National Historical Park, stepping in to serve as curator of the region's mining history. Tourism is now rebounding as buildings, ruins, shafts, and artifacts from the great copper mining era gradually open for public viewing. I've heard there are plans to one day incorporate the old mining sites alongside Torch Lake into the park's recreational and educational offerings. Some vegetation has returned to that shoreline already and new housing has cropped up, so things are progressing.

A little past Mason the road veers off slightly to the north, cutting through the village of Tamarack City and into the town of Hubbell, where the lights of the old IGA went out long ago. I always drive by the old Hubbell house too. My brother inherited the place, but he didn't want to live in it. He already owned a home. Some out-of-staters purchased it years ago, but they've yet to move in, so the place is lifeless and lonely. As tough as that is for me to see, it's even harder on my brother.

"Sometimes I wonder if I did the right thing," he said once in a moment of reflection. He was the third generation to have owned the home, and severing those ties wasn't easy.

"There's no sense hanging on to it if no one's gonna live in it," I said. "It costs too much to maintain."

"Maybe someday I'll buy it back."

There's a cemetery a few miles beyond Hubbell. It lies on the outskirts of Lake Linden, past the elementary school where I once played make-believe in the field, near the old carnival grounds along the lake. It sits on a quiet hillside a short distance from the site of Lakes Drive-In, the existence of which is only a memory now. In my younger years I wasn't able to go to the cemetery alone. It was a struggle to go there at all, really. There was too much grief underfoot, too much pain to process. In recent years I've overcome those constraints. What used to be painful for me is now a comfort—a bridge of some sort.

Whenever I reach its narrow entry, my car inches slowly up the smooth blacktop. I know what I'm looking for these days, though a few years ago I didn't have a clue how to find our family's graves. Katie taught me.

"Keep driving," she said as my vehicle crawled along beside headstones and fading silk flowers. "It's up the hill." Katie had never learned to drive, but she managed to make it out to the cemetery each year.

"How do you know where to find them?" I asked. I struggled at times to trust Katie's sense of direction; she was known to get off course. I struggled at times to trust Katie herself. This dynamic had developed when I was in my midthirties and the Great Mystery of the Disappearing Barbies was finally solved. It took Katie that long to admit she was the one who displaced them. She took them from my bedroom in 1980. She brought them to a neighbor's house trying to earn friends, where an unkind adolescent stole them from her in a ruthless game of keep-away. Things like that happened to Katie sometimes—kind friends were hard to come by. The case nearly empty, she carefully stashed it away where she found it. I wondered for years what happened to them. I'd even asked Ben if he did something with them. I'd called him the very afternoon I discovered them missing.

"Ben, did you to do something with my Barbies?" I asked that day, my tone accusatory.

"What do you mean?" he asked.

"They're all gone. The case is practically empty."

His voice rose. "Well, I didn't do anything. What would I have done with them?"

"They were there before. There were all in there. Maybe your nephew played with them?"

"Theresa, no one touched your stuff while it was here. I put it all upstairs the day I brought it home and that's where it's been the whole time. We didn't take your Barbie stuff."

The conversation ended coldly. In my distress I had insulted him. I had negated his kind gesture of safeguarding my things. I had injured the trust between us, as Katie had between herself and me. Such a breach is difficult to mend, but it mellows with time.

Katie and I continued inching our way along the cemetery lane. "Bev taught me how to find all the graves," she said. "She brings me here for Memorial Day." Bev was the friend Katie had always wanted. "It's right up here. Just a little further."

"Are you sure you know where we're going?"

"Yeah, Theresa. I know where I'm going. Up here." She scooted to the edge of the passenger seat and was staring out the window. "Hmm. I know it's up here somewhere." Things were not looking too promising when suddenly she pointed to the right. "There! Those two trees right there!" She sat back in her seat and flashed me a sanguine smile. "Bev said to look for the two pines, and she was right."

Now, as I roll along, I, too, look for the twin pines and park my vehicle at the edge of the lawn. I pick my way through the maze of mossy stones and weathered monuments until I come upon four granite markers flush to the ground and etched with a familiar name: Bertineau. It is here I find the gravestone of my brother, Stevie. There's an angel on his marker and the significant dates: October 5, 1960, and December 11, 1965.

Though it was too painful for Mom to talk with us about Stevie when we were young, she does now on occasion. The death of two sons, coupled with the loss of her husband so soon afterward, was the shadow of grief that plagued her all those years and darkened our childhood. The struggles of her youth and separation from her community compounded that grief. My adult awareness has allowed me to more justly process the transgressions of my parents, which as a child were painful and difficult to navigate. I realize now, as a wife and mother myself, the heartbreak Mom endured. Though replete forgiveness may still elude me, compassion does not.

While I was growing up, my brother's name brought to mind painful memories for my family, but Gramma once told me a funny tale about him and my father. One that rounded Stevie out for me, gave him dimension. I've always remembered it. I suppose that's why Gram told us her stories—so we'd never forget. "Your Dad was outside working," she said. "Little Stevie John went to check on him." She always called him that, *Little Stevie John*. "He was always fixin' cars, that dad o' yours. This one had a broken axel. All of a sudden, Stevie busted through the kitchen door laughing and singing:

'Daddy broke his asshole! Daddy broke his asshole!'"

Gram wore a tender grin and looked off toward the kitchen door as though she were reliving the moment, a habit of hers. "I don't know how he got his stories mixed up, but that Little Stevie John was such a funny little bugger," she said. "He could really make ya laugh." I wish I had been old enough to remember him.

Stevie was buried beside Grampa Bertineau, along with my first brother who died at birth. Somewhere beneath the sod lies a tiny metal plaque with the name *Baby Boy Bertineau*. He never had a headstone. Gramma's third daughter, Amanda, was buried there too. She died as a young adult of a congenital illness, her wake held in the parlor of the Mason house. Gramma's second daughter died during complications in late pregnancy. Her gravesite is unknown, though it's rumored she was buried somewhere in Mason.

Since plots were purchased in groups of four, our parents didn't have the money to buy a separate one for our brothers' burials when they passed. That's why they were buried with our grandparents. Once our father died, another plot had to be purchased further up the hill. He and Aunty Jean are together up there. She passed on a day we were certain *she* had chosen: July 4, 2005. And she wanted to come home—that's what her daughter said.

These days, in the Hubbell park, where Fourth of July picnics are held, there's a cedar swing overlooking the lake. Our cousins commissioned it in memory of their mother and in honor of the happy times their family shared during UP summer vacations. We sit there once in a while, look out across the lake, think about Aunty Jean. She will forever be a part of Independence Day.

The fourth stone in the lower plot belongs to Gramma. She was born May 8, 1911, and died of ovarian cancer on April 9, 1973. I'm in my early fifties now, and as I draw nearer to the age she was when she died, I find I compare myself to her more and more. I wonder what I will be like as a grandmother—if I will form the same bonds with my grandchildren as she formed with me, though I hope my grandchildren will not have the same need. When I struggle through a crisis I wonder if I finally understand how she might have felt all those years ago in a similar circumstance. Most importantly, I have come to realize how very short a time I had with her. She was fifty-one when I was born and within ten years she was gone. To a child, ten years is an eternity, but I know now it is but a brief measure of memories.

I kneel at her stone, pull the grass encroaching upon its face. Next time, I tell myself, bring some grass clippers. I place trinkets to decorate her gravesite: a ceramic angel, silk flowers. One year I purchased a four-pack of live pansies and with my fingers dug up the sandy soil around her marker and set the plants in the ground. Bunnies most likely chewed their tops off the same day, but I think my heart was in the right place.

I sit alone with her on the quiet hillside. The trees are still. Even the birds whisper. "I miss you, Gram," I say aloud. I kiss my fingertips and press them to her stone, look to the sky, cover my bases. "I think of you every day."

Since the trip to Arizona, I've come to realize Gramma did exactly as she promised that one winter day so many years ago. Somehow, through my dreams, through the slivers of culture, she found a way back—she was there for me when I needed her. As I brush the grass clippings from her headstone, I realize that I, too, have found a way to fulfill *my* promise.

Once again, I am her caretaker.

ABOUT THE AUTHOR

Born amidst the copper mining ruins of Michigan's Upper Peninsula, T. Marie Bertineau is of Anishinaabe-Ojibwe and French Canadian/Cornish descent. She is a member of the Keweenaw Bay Indian Community on the L'Anse Reservation, *migizi odoodeman*. Her work has appeared online with Minnesota's Carver County Arts Consortium; in *Mino Miikana*, a publication of the Native Justice Coalition and Waub Ajijaak Press; in the annual journal *U.P. Reader*; and is anthologized with the Chanhassen Writers Group of Minnesota. Married and the mother of two, she makes her home in the Great Lakes Region.

ACKNOWLEDGMENTS

This book could not have been written without the compassion, contributions, and encouragement of family. To Anne, Janie, Katie, and Chris: there are not enough thank yous to express how grateful I am for your understanding of my need to undertake this project, not only as a means of healing my own wounds but as a way of better understanding our history and our futures. To each of you as well as your families, my deepest love and devotion. To Mom: We are blessed with your wellbriety, with your presence here to this day. Thank you for your love, acceptance, and understanding and for venturing down this path with me. It could not have been easy for you, but you handled it with courage and empathy. Janie has always said you are a strong *kwe*.

To my husband and children: your love and support is my foundation. Thank you for allowing this self-absorption that is writing, for your permission to lose myself at the keyboard. Thank you for your understanding and tolerance, for reading and rereading, for supporting this lifelong goal. I know it's been a long journey, but I hope I've made you proud. You are my *ME*. You enrich my life in countless ways. I love you.

Thank you to my extended family: my uncles, aunties, and cousins who offered input, read drafts, and supported this project along the way. Thank you to Aunty Patsy for sharing her ma with us, for delving back into memory to add texture to this narrative. Thank you to Lisa for being a special part of my life story and for sharing this with Aunty Midge in her last year. Rest well, Aunty, and know that each of the Otten siblings was loved immensely. To Uncle Ray: thank you for taking part in this story and for your support and interest in my writing. Respect and gratitude to my cousin Scott for his kind input, and to Uncle Dan, our historian and mentor. I wish you were here to read the final product, Uncle. We would not be who we are without the love of you and Aunty Jean.

To the folks at the Chanhassen Writers Group: you were my fount. Your energy, enthusiasm, and love of writing was infectious. I had nothing but a seed when I sat down at your table. You provided the garden. Thank you for infusing me with commitment, ambition, and hope.

Special appreciation and acknowledgment to my friend and confidante Lori Lu, who across many years has always supported and encouraged me in my writing ventures and in life in general. You are the angel on my shoulder whispering *you can do it, you can do it*. Your positive affirmations did not fall on deaf ears.

Thank you to my posse—Carol, Marianne, Sue—who, through our treasured "whine" sessions, shared with me the joys and pitfalls of this publishing journey. Though I may have doubted myself, you kept the faith.

To my editors, Anne Jackson and Christine Neulieb, thank you. Anne, your skills and mentorship taught me so much about finding my voice and about seeking the most direct route to my reader wordwise. And Christine, thank you for recognizing the value of my story and for taking a chance on this debut writer. Your insight and care with my story is deeply appreciated.

Gratitude and respect to Debra Parrish of the Keweenaw Bay Indian Community for her generous contributions and oversight of the cultural aspects of my story. I embarked on this project with such limited knowledge but emerged with better understanding and confidence in my cultural awareness thanks in part to her guidance.

To all the folks at Lanternfish Press: I cannot think of a better place for this book, my word child. You are gentle and kind and in love with books for one reason: their stories. Thank you for helping me foster this one into existence. You've had to field a lot of questions from this newcomer, and you've done so with grace.

And to Katy Bresette and Jerry Jondreau: you both are such an inspiration. Thank you immensely for your guidance in customs and culture. I hope, when it comes time, that I do your teachings justice.

It is quite possible you are reading this book, in part, thanks to a program entitled #DVPit, a Twitter pitch event for marginalized voices. I offer the greatest respect for and appreciation to its creator, Beth Phelan, who works tirelessly to provide a safe, visible space for diverse voices.

Special mention to: Michigan Technological University Archives; the *Daily Mining Gazette*; Keweenaw National Historical Park; Pasty Central and Pasty.com; Keweenaw Bay Indian Community; Baraga County Historical Museum; Quincy Mine Hoist Association; Quincy Smelter Association; Department of Geological and Mining Engineering and Sciences of Michigan Technological University; the late Kevin E. Musser, creator of CopperRange.org; CopperCountryExplorer.com; the Diocese of Marquette; the Forest Service Office of the Ottawa National Forest; and the incomparable Carver County and Hennepin County library systems as well as the ever-vital Hancock and Dollar Bay public libraries. Appreciation also to Laurel Means, Dr. Anton Treuer, The Loft Literary Center, Kristi Belcamino, John Backman, and Robert Campbell.

Finally, to the lovely *Anishinaabekweg* of the KBIC Senior Center, *chi miigwech* for welcoming me to your table. *Miigwech* for your interest and encouragement in my book. By coincidence, you may find bits and pieces of your story here, too. If so, I hope I represented you well.